Martti Vainio, Juraj Šimko, Reijo Aulanko (Eds.)

HSCR 2017

Proceedings of the Second International Workshop on the History of Speech Communication Research

Helsinki, August 18-19, 2017

TUDpress

Studientexte zur Sprachkommunikation
Hg. von Rüdiger Hoffmann
ISSN 0940-6832
Bd. 83

Martti Vainio, Juraj Šimko, Reijo Aulanko (Eds.)

HSCR 2017

Proceedings of the Second International Workshop on the History of Speech Communication Research

Helsinki, August 18-19, 2017

TUDpress

2017

Cover image: Façade of the main building of the Imperial Alexander University of Finland (= University of Helsinki), 1870. Helsinki City Museum.

Bibliografische Information der Deutschen Nationalbibliothek
Die Deutsche Nationalbibliothek verzeichnet diese Publikation in der Deutschen Nationalbibliografie; detaillierte bibliografische Daten sind im Internet über http://dnb.d-nb.de abrufbar.

Bibliographic information published by the Deutsche Nationalbibliothek
The Deutsche Nationalbibliothek lists this publication in the Deutsche Nationalbibliografie; detailed bibliographic data are available in the Internet at http://dnb.d-nb.de.

ISBN 978-3-95908-097-2

Verlag der Wissenschaften
Bergstr. 70 | D-01069 Dresden
http://www.tudpress.de

Gesetzt von den Herausgebern.
Printed in Germany.

Preface

Following the inaugural event held in Dresden in 2015, the Second International Workshop on the History of Speech Communication Research (HSCR 2017) was held in August 2017 in Helsinki, Finland. The workshop was organized as a satellite event of Interspeech 2017 conference held in Stockholm, Sweden. The organizers received valuable assistance from the Special Interest Group (SIG) on *The History of Speech Communication Sciences*, from the *International Speech Communication Association* (ISCA) as well as from the organizers of the Interspeech 2017 conference.

The workshop was organized together with the new *Center for Digital Humanities* (HelDig) at the University of Helsinki. The Center serves as a Finnish research network and infrastructure focusing on solving research problems in humanities and social sciences using novel computational methods, and on studying digitalization as a phenomenon in its own right. Speech communication research is of course one of the prime examples of humanities enterprise relying heavily – and more and more – on state of the art digital methods, ranging from statistical modelling, through advanced signal processing methods to speech technology applications incorporating the latest deep-learning techniques. It was precisely this ongoing and accelerating methodological turn towards technology that acted as a special focus for the workshop: the changing face of speech communication research; from mechanical to digital.

This volume contains several important contributions addressing the evolution of speech sciences, notably experimental tools and methods. It includes studies of Kempelen's legendary "articulatory synthesizer" and other physical and computational models of speech production, development of the source-filter model of speech production as well as other important methodological advances essential to the field such as spectrography, notations and recording techniques.

The interest in the second installment of the workshop on the History of Speech Communication Research clearly supports the beliefs and hopes of the organizers of the inaugural event in Dresden that historical aspects of our field are of deep importance and should be studied with care and love. We express our strong belief that the Helsinki workshop will inspire many follow-up seminars in history of speech communication research.

Martti Vainio, Juraj Šimko and Reijo Aulanko
Helsinki, July 2017

Contents

THE DIGITAL HISTORY OF PHONETIC SCIENCE

Michael Ashby
Speech Hearing & Phonetic Sciences, University College London (UCL), UK
m.ashby@ucl.ac.uk

Abstract: This paper looks at the effects of the digital revolution on the activity of researching and writing the history of speech communication research. Examples are given from the author's recent work in which new findings flow from the application of digital methods which may now seem commonplace but have come into use only within the last twenty years. Consideration is then given to the widely-held notion that 'digital history' is defined by its use of 'big data'. It is shown that large corpora such as Google Books and the Internet Archive already benefit our efforts as historians of speech communication research, although we should make efforts to augment those databases, or build specialised databases of our own, with materials which target our requirements more directly. That would in turn entail developing OCR to deal with IPA and other phonetic symbols, and an indication is given of how that can be achieved. In conclusion it is suggested that digital methods radically reduce the cost in time and resources of lines of inquiry which would previously have seemed impracticable, thus changing our perspectives on what can and should be attempted and giving us the freedom to be more adventurous in our investigations.

1 Introduction

The special focus for this workshop was announced as 'the changing face of speech communication research; from mechanical to digital', and of course the organisers primarily had in mind the enormous and accelerating changes which digital technology has brought in speech research over the last 50 years. But the theme of this paper is that the 'digital revolution' is not merely an aspect of our subject-matter. In fact, the same digital revolution is transforming the discipline of history itself, and profound changes are affecting how any of us go about studying and presenting the history of our subject, regardless of whether our specialist field be ancient or modern.

We are meeting today in HELDIG, Helsinki's new Centre for Digital Humanities. Within the range of digital humanities, 'digital history' is already an established discipline—though both for digital humanities as a whole and digital history in particular there is a wide ranging debate about their definition. But before trying to say anything about digital history in general, or asking whether there is or can be a 'digital history' of speech communication research, I will begin with some specific examples from my own recent research on the period 1890–1940 [3], calling attention to the way in which digital tools have facilitated the work.

2 Digital data and tools for the history of phonetic science

2.1 The Cardinal Vowel X-rays

Everyone now recognizes that digital imaging has had a revolutionary impact in almost every sphere of art and science, and it is strange to reflect that less than 20 years ago librarians and archivists were still debating its potential roles in preservation and access [8]. We will begin with a simple example where a research finding in the history of phonetic science has been facilitated at every step by digital image processing.

The year 2017 is the centenary of Daniel Jones's Cardinal Vowel system, and Figure 1 reproduces a composite print of the celebrated X-rays of vowel positions he made when the system was devised. This image was re-photographed digitally by the author from the original held in the Daniel Jones Papers, UCL Special Collections, housed at the time of the photograph in the National Archives at Kew. It is worth noting that only within the last decade, self-access digital photography has become the norm in our great libraries and archives.

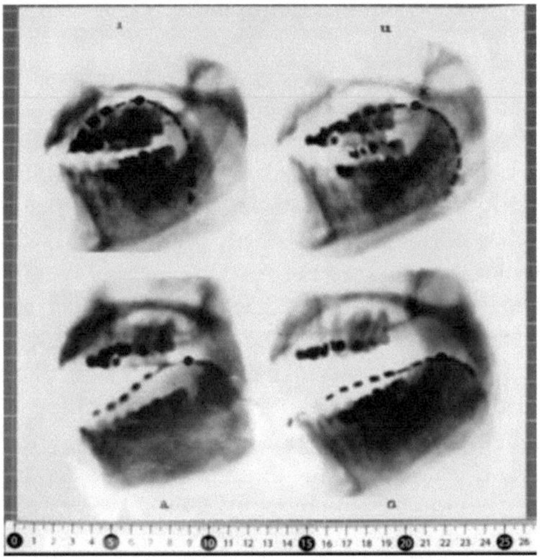

Figure 1. The composite positive print (probably *c.* 1930) of Daniel Jones's Cardinal Vowel X-rays made in 1917 (re-photographed digitally by the author from the original held in the Daniel Jones Papers, UCL Special Collections).

The original X-rays were made in 1917, but it is probably not widely realized that having included some of them in his papers of 1917 and 1918, Jones did not then republish any of the X-rays for more than 30 years. They eventually reappeared in the form of the familiar frontispiece, initially in his smaller work *The Pronunciation of English*, 3rd edition (1950) and then finally in the reprint of the eighth edition of the *Outline of English Phonetics* in 1957, by which time they were 40 years old. Moreover, the X-ray of Cardinal Vowel number 4, [a], though it had been made in 1917 like the others, did not appear anywhere until the 1950 frontispiece—and up to that point was not even acknowledged to exist.

There must have been a reason for the long delay in its publication, and presumably Jones considered some aspect of the [a] image unsatisfactory. Examination of the four X-rays suggests that the problem might lie in the velopharyngeal area. It appears that a considerable portion has been masked off the right-hand edge of [a] compared with the other images. It is unclear whether any part of the remaining image for [a] corresponds to the velum—but if the shadow at top right does indicate the velum, it appears to be in a lowered position. The purpose of cropping the image may be to conceal this—or perhaps to conceal just how closely the tongue root is approaching the rear pharynx wall. The visual indication of apparent nasality would conflict with Jones's characterisation of the vowel as 'oral' (not nasalised), and a narrow constriction in the pharynx would conflict with his characterisation of the vowel as 'open'.

The accurate tracing of images would once have required specialist graphic skills and equipment, but is now easily accomplished digitally using a line-drawing tool on a transparent layer in a Photoshop document. Similarly, superimposition of tracings is easily done by using a stack of such transparent layers. Superimposed tracings were therefore made of the velum as visible in the [i], [u] and [ɑ] images, and the resulting combined tracing placed over the [a] image. The result is shown in Figure 2, from which it is evident that an extensive portion of the image of the pharynx must have been removed from [a]—enough to conceal a considerable degree of velum lowering, if that were indeed the motivation. We thus have a simple example where digital techniques which are now commonplace facilitate the forensic revaluation of research images which are a century old.

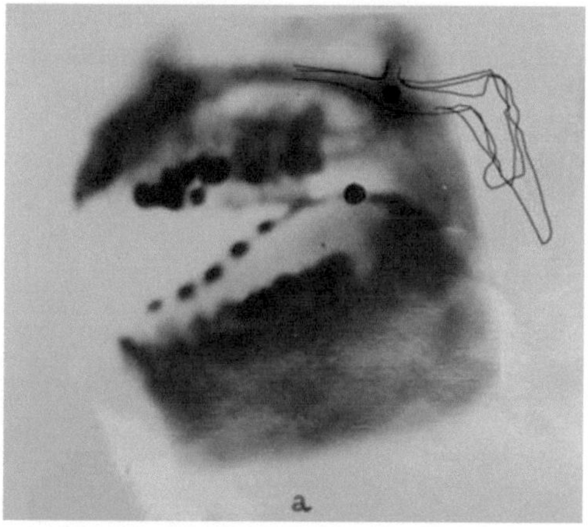

Figure 2. Daniel Jones's X-ray image of Cardinal Vowel 4, [a], overlaid with outline tracings of the velum position from Cardinal Vowels [i ɑ u].

2.2 Paget's estimates of vowel resonances

As with digital imaging, so digital techniques have revolutionised the recording and processing of sound for almost every purpose. For speech researchers, the most important application is of course the analysis of speech corpora [5]. At the same time, digital preservation and distribution make it possible to analyse legacy recordings as easily as those newly made. Even the very earliest acoustic recordings, whether on cylinder or disc, can furnish useful fundamental frequency data [3]. With the advent of electrical recording from 1925, very satisfactory formant tracking becomes possible. A particularly interesting category of recordings in the present context are those which can potentially corroborate descriptions or analyses published in the past. We will give an example bearing on the auditory analysis of vowel quality.

In the pre-spectrographic era, numerous observers published values for 'vowel resonances'—in modern terms, formant frequencies—estimated auditorily. Among the most sophisticated were those of Sir Richard Paget (1869–1955). Paget unhesitatingly identified two resonances in all vowels (including those back vowels where others had found a single resonance), and displayed his results graphically in a way that enabled their orderly relationship to vowel articulation to be taken in at a glance. His chart of resonances was first published in 1922 [11] and was to reappear many times in his publications; Figure 3 reproduces the final version from his book *Human Speech* of 1930 [12].

Paget's results have been certainly recognised as remarkable anticipations of what would later be broadly confirmed by instrumental methods. We can see at once that his resonances are estimates of F_1 and F_2, and in general of the right order of magnitude for a male speaker. But the question seems never to have been addressed of whether they might in fact be precise estimates of Paget's own formant frequencies. It was decided to investigate the matter by searching for a recording of Paget from which an acoustic analysis could be attempted.

The catalogue of the British Library Sound Archive revealed a single recording of Paget, 3m 25s in duration, and evidently a tape transfer from a 78 rpm disc original. The accompanying metadata is incomplete, but the recording can be dated from the content to approximately 1930. A digitized copy was opened in SFS [6] for analysis using *formanal*, a formant tracker based on LPC polynomial roots and dynamic programming. The recording was manually annotated to select sampling points in as many tokens as possible of each vowel type. Using Wells's standard lexical sets [13] to identify vowels, the numbers of tokens annotated were DRESS 15, FLEECE 11, FOOT 4, GOOSE 4, KIT 6, LOT 12, NURSE 11, SCHWA 5, START 10, STRUT 9, THOUGHT 12, TRAP 15. A script written in Speech Measurement Language (SML) [6] was used to collect the F_1 and F_2 estimates from the 124 annotation points, and these were plotted on a logarithmic scale of frequency in such a way that they could be superimposed directly on Paget's figure for comparison. The result appears in Figure 4.

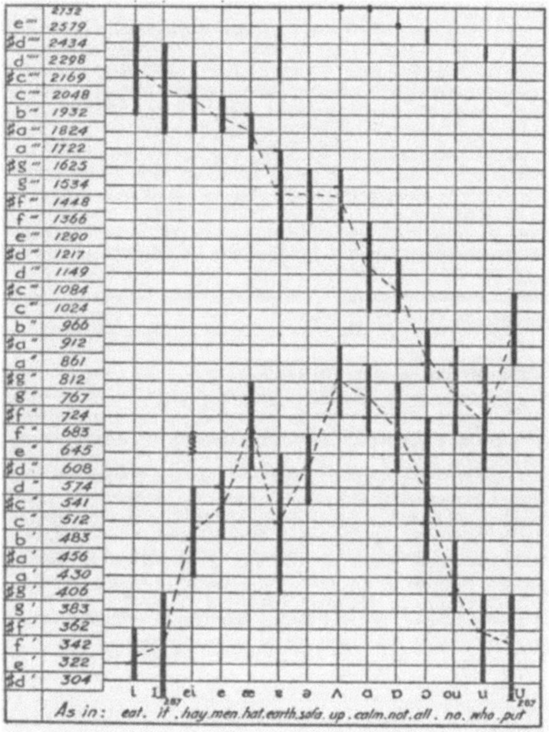

Figure 3. Frequencies of the resonances in English (RP) vowels, as heard by Paget [12: p.86]. The vertical bars indicate the range of observed variation.

Since the main focus of the present discussion is on the digital tools employed, only a brief discussion can be offered here of the results obtained. Figure 4 reveals an impressive degree of agreement between Paget's auditory estimates and those made automatically. The correspondence is especially remarkable for F_2, where the great majority of all the observed values lie within the ranges specified by Paget. But across the board the F_1 estimates extracted automatically are somewhat lower than those given by Paget, with the result that the frequency scale of his figure has had to be extended downwards by a further 5 semitones to accommodate them. In accounting for this, two main factors may be mentioned. First, Paget's estimates were made on whispered vowels, whereas the automatic analysis was carried out on a recording of normal phonated speech. A range of studies have reported higher F_1 in whispered speech than in phonated speech [9]. Second, Paget was listening to sustained vowels in isolation, whereas the instrumental estimates have been made on running speech, in which the target configurations were potentially subject to undershoot (e.g., in degree of jaw opening for open vowels). It is entirely possible, therefore, that Paget's estimates were precisely accurate for the sustained whispered vowels he was analysing, and the real mismatch is between those decontextualized vowels and the vowels he produced in running speech.

It may be worth reminding ourselves how many digital tools and techniques played a role in obtaining this result. The recording of Paget was located by searching a digital library catalogue. A digital audio file was supplied by file transfer. Digital tools were used to display and annotate the file and to track the formants. More digital tools were used to collect and process the results, and then digital image processing was used to overlay the findings on Paget's original figure.

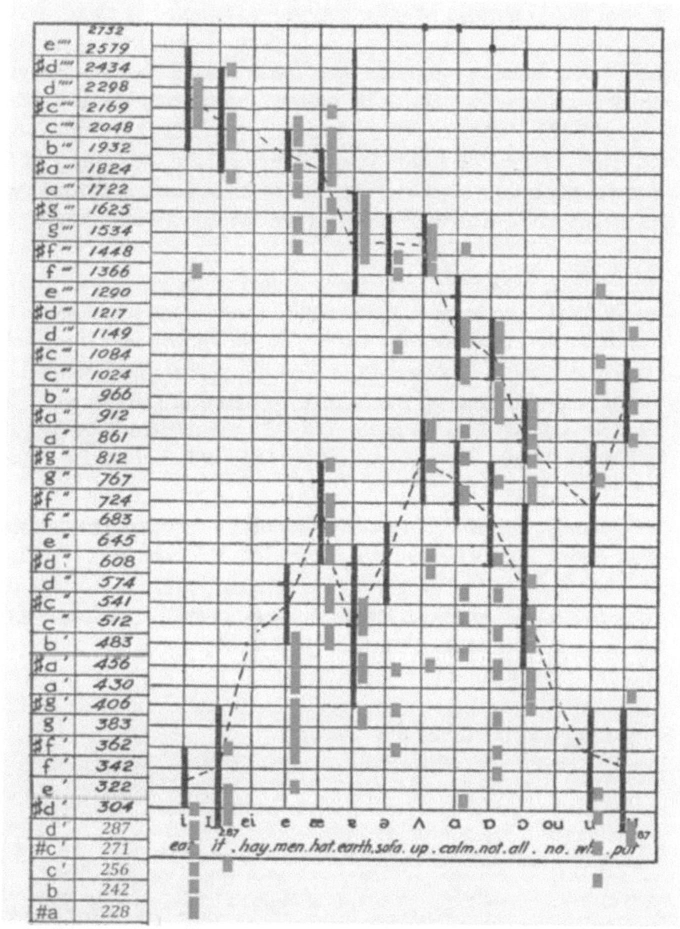

Figure 4. Automatically extracted estimates of F_1 (blue) and F_2 (orange) plotted on Paget's figure for comparison with his auditory estimates. The frequency scale has had to be extended downwards by 5 semitones to accommodate the lowest F_1 observations.

2.3 General purpose tools

Finally, though they have become so familiar that we are in danger of taking them entirely for granted, we should remind ourselves of numerous general purpose digital tools that have greatly facilitated the work of the historian. As examples we can point to online civil records (births, marriages, deaths, census returns, etc.), digital newspaper archives, the digitized archives of major scientific journals (such as *Nature*), and library catalogues, especially union catalogues such WorldCat [17]. Probably the single most indispensable tool in academic work of any kind has become bibliographic software such as Zotero [18].

3 Digital history

The examples just cited certainly illustrate the use of digital tools and techniques, but does the result merit the label 'digital history'? In fact, what *is* digital history?

3.1 'Big data' and digital history of science

Perhaps the single most prominent and widely shared notion about digital history is that it makes use of unprecedented amounts of information—so called 'big data'. As a *Nature* article put it, paraphrasing Jürgen Renn (*b*. 1956), the idea in digital history is that 'all possible sources of information that have come down over the millennia should be digitized and made available in a form that allows the data to be mined beyond traditional barriers of language and academic discipline' [1]. Historians of science (such as Renn himself) have certainly been to the fore in developing the general field of digital history, but the history of speech communication science forms only a tiny corner of the history of science, and as yet we would find it impossible to point to any collection of 'big data' assembled with our specific needs in mind.

3.2 Data and the history of speech communication research

Study of the history of speech communication research is of course assisted to some degree by the growth of general purpose data sources, for the simple reason that if sufficient data is digitized, more and more material of interest to us will necessarily be included. Various online repositories now hold many billions of pages of digitized text [14]. A very large number of printed books (one estimate puts it at 30 million) have been digitized by Google, and a subset of these forms the Google Books Ngram collection [10], probably the best known dataset for charting word usage over time.

The example Ngram in Figure 5 shows how mentions of 'phonetics laboratory' peak in the late 1960s before beginning a decline, while mentions of 'computer' continue to rise. This seems to illustrate very well that from the 1970s onwards more and more of the functions which had once required special-purpose laboratory apparatus were taken over by computers. We notice also the deep trough centred around 1950 in the curve for 'phonetics laboratory', which surely shows the prolonged effect of the Second World War, the recovery around 1960 corresponding nicely with the resumption of the International Congresses of Phonetic Science (the first postwar meeting was in Helsinki in 1961).

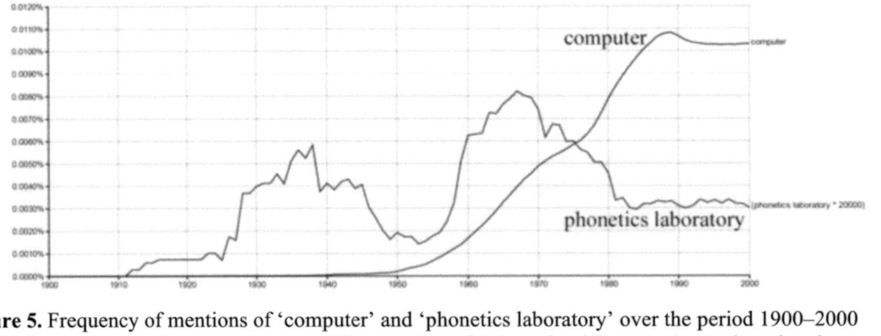

Figure 5. Frequency of mentions of 'computer' and 'phonetics laboratory' over the period 1900–2000 in the Google Books Ngram collection. (The number of 'phonetics laboratory' mentions has been scaled by 20000).

While this is very suggestive, we have to concede that we do not know how much of the relevant speech-research literature is included in the Google Books Ngram collection. The Google Books database has also been criticised for the apparent unreliability of its metadata.

In a random sample of 400, [7] found metadata errors in almost 37% of books; errors specifically affecting date of publication were present in almost 1 in 10.

While the Google Books initiative appears to be losing momentum, the Internet Archive [15] by contrast continues to grow (it presently claims 11 million volumes), and would probably now be any historian's first recourse in the search for, say, a nineteenth-century scholarly work or journal. Whether we want to read Willis's seminal 1829 paper on vowels, Merkel's great *Anthropophonik* of 1857, Rousselot's revolutionary doctoral thesis of 1891, or countless items far more obscure, a few clicks will bring us a digital version—and it will be more useful to us than a dusty copy brought out of the library bookstack, since in general it will have been through OCR and the text will therefore be searchable. Hitherto, the search facilities over the Internet Archive database have worked only on metadata, but a 'search full text of books' across the whole database has recently been added 'in beta'—and initial trials with it seem very promising.

3.3 Building and using specific HSCR databases

As for assembling special-purpose text corpora more suited to our needs, there are in principle low-cost tools for compiling them, and for mining the collected data. Paper Machines [16] is open-source software that works in conjunction with Zotero. According to the description provided on its home page, its purpose is 'to allow individual researchers to generate analyses and visualizations of user-provided corpora, without requiring extensive computational resources or technical knowledge'. It would be encouraging to see the HSCR community making attempts along these lines. We could, for example, think of building a database from the issues of an early journal such as *Phonetische Studien* or from the successive volumes of Proceedings of ICPhS.

3.4 OCR for phonetic symbols

With either of these examples, we would, however, encounter a problem, since scattered throughout them is text in phonetic transcription which will defeat standard Optical Character Recognition (OCR) software. In other material which we would certainly want to include, the problem is more severe. For instance, the *Journal of the International Phonetic Association* exists in digital form only as far back as 1971. Prior to that, for more than 80 years in its former guise as *Le Maître Phonétique*, the whole journal was printed in phonetic transcription. Unless we can solve the problem of OCR for phonetic symbols, any attempt at the data-mining of phonetic literature (or literature such as dictionaries, which incorporate phonetic symbols alongside conventional text) is likely to produce results peppered with garbage.

Though no current OCR system appears to cater off-the-shelf for phonetic symbols, research reported in [4] shows that at least one relatively inexpensive commercial system can be trained to handle text in IPA symbols, producing a Unicode output that is more than 99% accurate (reckoned by word). See Figure 6.

There seems to be no obstacle in principle, then, to the development of special corpora for HSCR purposes, whether linked to specific projects or shared as a general resource.

4 Summary and conclusions

In summary, therefore, we can say that work on the history of speech communication science is already benefiting from some of the developments widely regarded as most characteristic of 'digital history', and there is no impediment in principle to the creation of our own special purpose databases enabling us to reap those benefits more fully. At the same time, since speech research involves objects such as images and audio which are fully as important as text, the focused application of digital tools on those data types gives a dimension to our work which historians in other fields will not necessarily share.

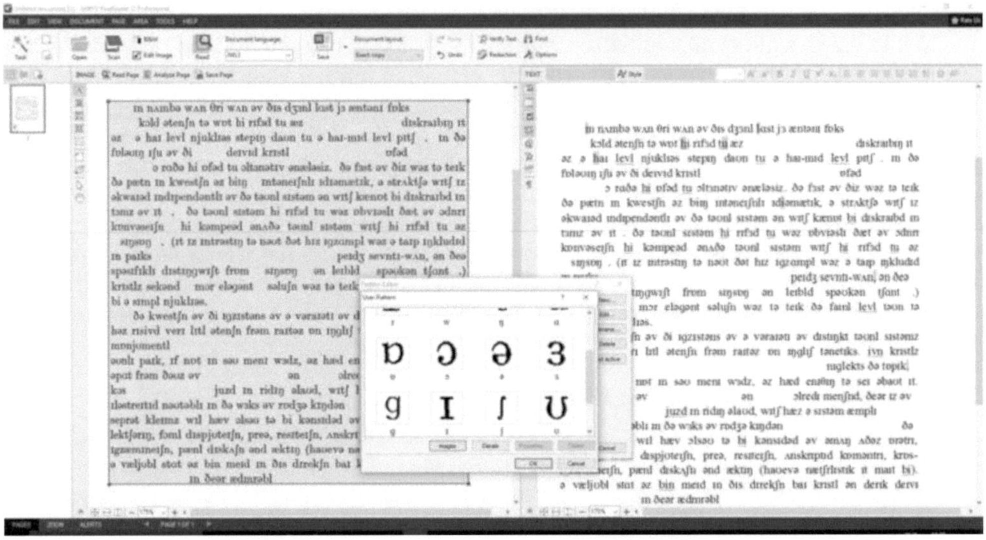

Figure 6. A screenshot from ABBYY FineReader showing training in progress for OCR of phonetic symbols. At left, the original image; at right the interim recognition output. The small overlaid window shows the user-defined patterns which are in the process of being interactively developed.

It is debateable to what extent digital tools and methods make possible anything which was unrealisable previously. Given sufficient time and resources, we could, for instance, have compared Jones's Cardinal Vowel images using conventional photographic and graphic techniques at any time over the last century. Similarly, though it would have been laborious to do so, we could have assessed Paget's vowel resonances with the analog technology of fifty years ago. Either project would have required to be funded with at least a small grant, justified by a research proposal. But digital approaches change costs radically, even if what they make possible was technically possible in principle by analogue means. The change in cost in turn changes our perspectives: lines of inquiry that would previously have seemed too complex or expensive to pursue can now be followed on a whim, out of curiosity, and without a need to seek justification for expenditure of resources. The resulting freedom licenses more experimentation—and even playfulness—in our investigations, and, when we are lucky, can lead us to serendipitous discoveries we could have made no other way.

5 References

[1] A. Abbott, 'Digital history', *Nature*, vol. 409, no. 6820, pp. 556–557, Feb. 2001.

[2] M. G. Ashby, 'Experimental phonetics at University College London before World War I', in *HSCR 2015: proceedings of the First International Workshop on the History of Speech Communication Research, Dresden, September 4-5, 2015*, R. Hoffmann and J. Trouvain, Eds. Dresden: TUDpress, 2015, pp. 118–127.

[3] M. G. Ashby, 'Experimental phonetics in Britain, 1890-1940', DPhil, Oxford, 2016.

[4] M. G. Ashby, 'Recognition where it's due: Some experiments in optical character recognition (OCR) for phonetic symbols', *Journal of the English Phonetic Society of Japan*, vol. 21, pp. 63–79, 2017.

[5] J. Harrington, *Phonetic analysis of speech corpora*. Chichester ; Malden, Mass.: Wiley-Blackwell, 2010.

[6] M. Huckvale, 'Speech Filing System', 2013. [Online]. Available: http://www.phon.ucl.ac.uk/resource/sfs/. [Accessed: 20-Mar-2015].

[7] R. James and A. Weiss, 'An assessment of Google Books' metadata', *Journal of Library Metadata*, vol. 12, no. 1, pp. 15–22, Jan. 2012.

[8] Joint National Preservation Office and Research Libraries Group Preservation Conference, Ed., *Guidelines for digital imaging.* London: National Preservation Office, The British Library, 1998.

[9] K. J. Kallail and F. W. Emanuel, 'Formant-frequency differences between isolated whispered and phonated vowel samples produced by adult female subjects', *Journal of Speech and Hearing Research*, vol. 27, no. 2, pp. 245–51, 1984.

[10] J.-B. Michel *et al.*, 'Quantitative analysis of culture using millions of digitized books', *Science*, vol. 331, no. 6014, pp. 176–182, Jan. 2011.

[11] R. A. S. Paget, *Vowel resonances*. London: International Phonetic Association, 1922.

[12] R. A. S. Paget, *Human speech: Some observations, experiments, and conclusions as to the nature, origin, purpose and possible improvement of human speech*. London: K. Paul, Trench, Trubner & Co, 1930.

[13] J. C. Wells, *Accents of English*. Cambridge: Cambridge University Press, 1982.

[14] 'The world as seen through books: Comparing the Internet Archive, HathiTrust, and Google Books Ngrams Collections', *GDELT Blog*, 02-Oct-2015. [Online]. Available: http://blog.gdeltproject.org/ [Accessed: 31-May-2017].

[15] 'Internet Archive: Digital library of free books, movies, music & Wayback Machine'. [Online]. Available: https://archive.org/index.php. [Accessed: 10-Jun-2017].

[16] 'Paper Machines | Visualize your Zotero collections'. [Online]. Available: http://papermachines.org/. [Accessed: 31-May-2017].

[17] 'WorldCat.org: The world's largest library catalog'. [Online]. Available: https://www.worldcat.org/. [Accessed: 10-Jun-2017].

[18] 'Zotero | Home'. [Online]. Available: https://www.zotero.org/. [Accessed: 10-Jun-2017].

Editing Kempelen's "Mechanismus der menschlichen Sprache": Experiences and Findings

Fabian Brackhane[1], *Richard Sproat*[2], *Jürgen Trouvain*[3]
[1]*Institut für Deutsche Sprache, Mannheim, Germany,* [2]*Google Research, New York, USA,*
[3]*Saarland University, Saarbrücken, Germany*
brackhane@ids-mannheim.de

Abstract: Wolfgang von Kempelen's book "The Mechanism of Human Speech" from 1791 is a famous milestone in the history of speech communication research. It has an enormous relevance for the phonetic sciences and it marks an important turning point for the development of the (mechanical) speech synthesis. So far no English version of this work was available, which excludes many interested researchers. Access to the original versions in German and French is restricted for various reasons. For example the blackletter script of the German version is troublesome for most of today's readers. We report here on a new edition of Kempelen's book which unites a better readable German version and its English translation. It will now also be in a searchable electronic format and has been enriched with many commentaries, which aid in the understanding of details of the late 18th century that are little known or unknown to many researchers today.

1 Introduction

Scientific discussion about speech goes far into history. Already from antiquity we know of scholars like the Greek physician Galen who dealt with the production of speech and its physiological basis. During the Middle Ages less empirical but extensively philosophical and theosophical-based approaches dominated. Still in the 18th century theories were discussed that postulated that speech is a gift of God, often based on crude physiological "findings". At the same time the age of enlightenment settled down more and more so that empirical approaches to science became more common. In this period of scientific tension Kempelen's book was published.

In the history of science there are probably few persons whose work has been so varyingly judged over the centuries like that of Wolfgang von Kempelen. Although he himself was often referred to as a fraud, his book, released in 1791, was soon called a "classic" work [1: 84; 2: 316].

An intensive study of this seemingly "antiquated" work shows for instance that many theories of speech production (which could be verified by using modern technology) were already drafted long ago on the basis of "primitive" but nevertheless precise observation. Especially in contrast to contemporary publications, Kempelen's "Mechanismus" is a prime example of early empirical science that achieved very amazing results from today's perspective.

Having been a phonetic standard reference for many decades, the fame of the book has survived until today. In 1970 a very precise facsimile printing was edited by Herbert E. Brekle and Wolfgang Wildgen [3]. Due to the progressive digitalization of the last few years electronic versions of the text became easily available via the internet. But all these means of access did not eliminate the fundamental obstacles in reading and understanding this exceptional milestone of basic phonetic sciences.

Kempelen's book was published in German and French in parallel. Today, both versions are partially hard to understand because of their old-fashioned diction and lack of knowledge about the contemporary context. In addition, readers of the German edition have to be familiar with blackletter (or Gothic) script. An English translation of the book that makes it accessible for a really broad readership has been completely missing until now. The authors were often told by international colleagues that they had heard much about Kempelen's famous book but that they were not able to read it themselves. For this reason the authors decided to issue a new edition of this book which is central for the understanding of language research in the 18th century [4]. The edition contains a transliterated and commented version of the German original as well as a close translation into English. This paper presents some experiences and findings on the content of the "Mechanismus" that we made during the editing process.

2 Wolfgang von Kempelen

Kempelen's biography is quite prototypical for outstanding scholars of the age of enlightenment. He was a professional manager and a gifted mechanic, a brilliant magician and a sober naturalist, and not least one whose reputation has in posterity been romantically mystified, confused and accused of charlatanism. Due to a lack of work with primary sources and deficits in research, some of the "facts" on his life and work, which have now been proven as legends, find their way even to today's publications (see Reininger [5, 6] for a detailed and precise biography of Kempelen). Here we concentrate on a few central points.

Kempelen was born on January 23, 1734 in the then Austrian city of Pressburg (today Bratislava, Slovakia). He received an education in philosophy and law. From 1755 to 1798 he had a career as a civil servant at the Hungarian court chamber. Besides his official administrative duties he dealt with several technical improvements and innovations such as various water lifting mechanisms, a mobile bed, and a mechanical typing device for blind people. Best known of his inventions are his steam engines and the spectacular and today infamous "mechanical chess player" which served as the namesake for Amazon's *Mechanical Turk* (a web service that allows for crowd sourcing of tasks that humans excel at, but which are still difficult for machines). We focus here on his speaking machine described in his book "Mechanismus der menschlichen Sprache nebst der Beschreibung seiner sprechenden Maschine" from 1791 [3].

3 The "Mechanismus der menschlichen Sprache"

The motivation of Kempelen's book, its title and concept are not widely known. This is not surprising because Kempelen himself did not say anything about his motivation. Reading the full title of Kempelen's book[1] leaves the impression of a textbook on speech production with a short and less important appendix on the "speaking machine". In fact, it is exactly the other way around: The whole book was conceptualized to make the final description of the speaking machine understandable and to underpin its design.

When Kempelen first presented his "speaking machine" in 1783 he was massively criticized and accused of presenting yet another fraud following on his "mechanical chess player"[2,3]. For this reason he decided to disclose the construction of his speech synthesis device. But to make his readers understand his truly serious construction he firstly had to present his underlying physiological findings. It has sometimes been objected that Kempelen mostly compiled already published statements about speech production and presented few of

---

[1] "Wolfgang von Kempelen Imperial-royal Court Councillor's Mechanism of Human Speech along with the Description of his Speaking Machine. With 27 Copper Plates."

[2] This actual was just as little a fraud than the "speaking machine" but just misunderstood like that.

[3] Cf. the prototypical polemic of the anonymous author "Rm", that shows very well the outrage as well as the fundamental misunderstanding of the "speaking machine" [7].

his own findings. But this method was imperative because he had to rely on already accepted authors to give more power to his own argumentation.

The book is divided into five chapters of very different scope:

I. On speech in general. (27 pp.)

II. Thoughts on the questions: Whether language was discovered by humans, or whether it was created for them? Whether all language originated from a single language? (29 pp.)

III. On the organs of speech and their function. (121 pp.)

IV. On the sounds or letters of the European languages. (210 pp.)

V. On the speaking machine. (69 pp.)

In addition, the book is equipped with remarkable illustrations on 27 copper plates that were made by Kempelen himself.

Kempelen had already announced his publication in 1784 and we do not know why he needed seven years to finish the book. But there are some hints. Firstly, Kempelen was very busy with his administrative duties in that time. Secondly, the scope of the book was enlarged by and by. Presumably to achieve a broader reception, the book finally was published in German and French in parallel (Fig. 1). Though there is no evidence, it seems likely that the translation into French was made by Kempelen himself. Also nothing is known about the exact circulation of the book, but a number of about 250 copies can be indirectly assumed.

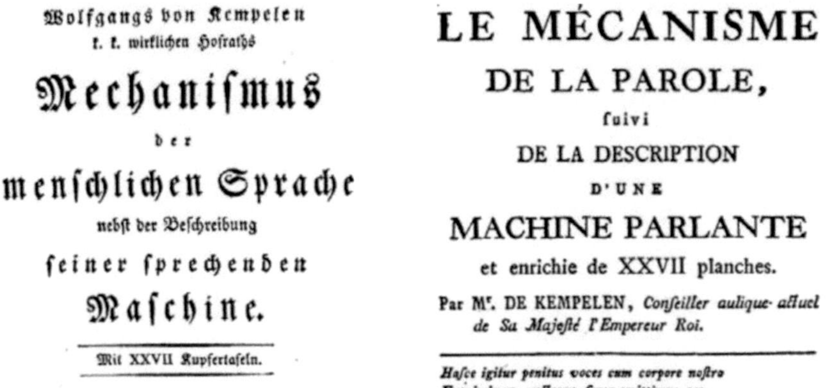
Wolfgangs von Kempelen
k. k. wirklichen Hofraths
Mechaniſmus
der
menſchlichen Sprache
nebſt der Beſchreibung
ſeiner ſprechenden
Maſchine.
Mit XXVII Kupfertafeln.

Haſce igitur penitus voces cum corpore noſtro
Exprimimus, rectoque foras emittimus ore,
Mobilis articulat verborum dædala lingua,
Formaturaque labrorum pro parte figurat.
Lucret. lib. IV. v. 533.

Wien,
bei J. V. Degen, 1791.

LE MÉCANISME
DE LA PAROLE,
ſuivi
DE LA DESCRIPTION
D'UNE
MACHINE PARLANTE
et enrichie de XXVII planches.
Par Mr. DE KEMPELEN, *Conſeiller aulique-actuel de Sa Majeſté l'Empereur Roi.*

Haſce igitur penitus voces cum corpore noſtro
Exprimimus, rectoque foras emittimus ore,
Mobilis articulat verborum dædala lingua,
Formaturaque labrorum pro parte figurat.
Lucret. lib. IV. v. 533.

À VIENNE,
Imprimé chez B. Bauer,
& ſe trouve
chez J. V. Degen 1791.

Figure 1. Title pages of the German and French original edition of Kempelen's book.

While in chapters 1–4 Kempelen partially compiled contemporary sources and discussed them, the last chapter of his book is completely his own work. Here, Kempelen describes the construction of his speaking machine as well as its genesis. His frank report on his problematic first prototypes that were less anatomically based is remarkable. The level of detail in the description of his final machine is as surprising as the fact that some rather important measures, e.g. for the bellows or the reed pipe, were missing. Nonetheless Kempelen's ground-breaking approach to mechanical speech synthesis is clearly visible, and this was enhanced by his presentation of nine to-scale figures of the mechanism.

4 The New Edition

The goal of our work was to facilitate the approach and the understanding of Kempelen's book for today's readers as much as possible but without eliminating its essential characteristics. As much meta-information related to the original printing as possible had to be preserved. For that we decided to make a bilingual edition that offers an only typographically "modernized" version of the German original and an English translation. Every double page of the new edition corresponds to one single page of Kempelen's book in these two variants.

For the German version we decided to replace the black letter by a modern Antiqua type (such as Times New Roman). But Antiqua was already used in the original edition for non-German terms and for explicit examples. Those terms now were typeset in *italics*. Texts printed in black letter show some variation in font size for emphasizing. This was replaced by **bold** font style.

The original pagination was prefixed to the text block on the left. The modern editorial pagination was put at the end of the page. The German and the French versions of the "Mechanism" are fundamentally identical in their content but differ in details from one another. For instance, representations of some words or syllables in given examples have not always the same spelling. In these cases we added the French versions.

Kempelen expected his readers to generally be familiar with quotations from Latin and Greek classics. That is why he often quoted these in a rather careful way or – especially with longer citations – only gave the gist of them; also the references often are provided only cursorily. To facilitate today's readers' understanding of the argumentation linked to these quotations, these were completed to their full text and translated into German where necessary.

We intensively discussed how to incorporate our editorial comments into the text without disturbing the flow too much. Because of their very heterogeneous nature we decided on a two-part strategy: Short explanations of a phrase were placed as marginal notes on the outer page margin.[4] More detailed explanations such as biographical dates and notes on quotes were placed as footnotes at the very end of every page.

The excellent digitization by the Saxon State and University Library in Dresden served as a source for the illustrations.

5 English Translation

For a modern native speaker of German Kempelen's text is not easy to understand, and it is even harder of course for a second language speaker. But even in cases where his meaning is clear, finding the right way to express it in English that at least tries to convey the same nuances can be a challenge. One of the additional challenges with an old text like this is picking the right register. Ideally, one might have tried to translate into 18th Century English, but as this would likely be a challenge even for a professional translator, we arrived at the

---

[4] Sometimes Kempelen's wording is so different from its usage today that a comparison with the (original) French version was also helpful for a native speaker of German to understand the German version.

following compromise: namely to translate into modern English, but to try to avoid modern phonetic terminology where possible. Thus, for example, for his *Zungenkanal*, which clearly corresponds to our modern notion of *vocal tract*, the modern term was replaced by the translation *tongue channel*. We cannot exclude errors of consistency despite a thorough rereading of the translation after its completion, but if any such inconsistencies remain, they can be attributed to the long period over which the translation was done.

One fortunate feature of the modern age is of course the rapid access to a whole range of information. Never once was a print dictionary used, always online sources, including of course Wikipedia and Google Books, especially where it was needed to find interpretations of obscure technical terms. But first and foremost heavy use of Google Machine Translation (GMT) was made. While this technology has improved much, especially recently, it is of course still not possible to use it to translate most texts without a fair amount of post editing. This is even more true for older texts such as Kempelen's. However it still proved very useful in helping suggest appropriate translations for words and short phrases, and for that purpose it was extensively used. This point fits well into a historical approach to language and speech technology from the 18th Century, including the work of Kempelen, right up to the digital speech and language systems of the 21st Century, of which GMT is one such instance [8]. GMT is, in fact, a natural descendant of Kempelen's work on understanding human speech, and it is only fitting that it should now be used to help make Kempelen's pioneering efforts accessible to a broader audience.

Figure 2 shows as an example page 57 of the German original print and its commented translation.

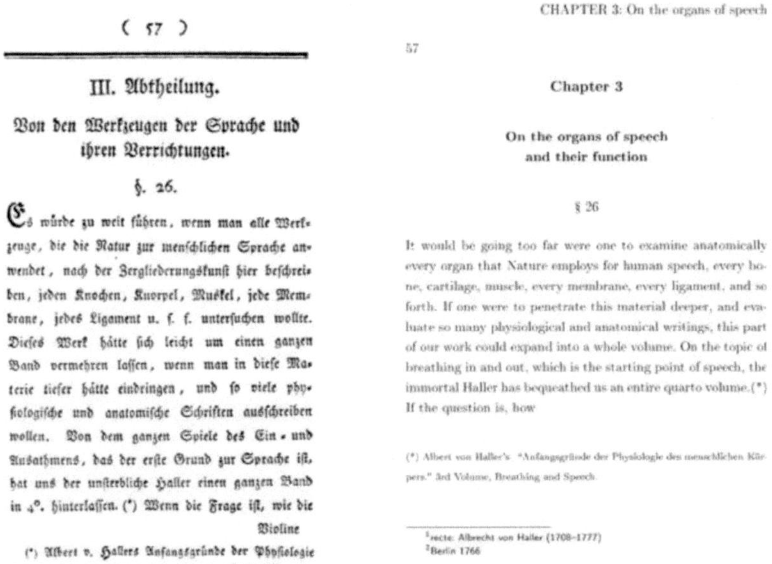

(57)

III. Abtheilung.

Von den Werkzeugen der Sprache und ihren Verrichtungen.

§. 26.

Es würde zu weit führen, wenn man alle Werkzeuge, die die Natur zur menschlichen Sprache anwendet, nach der Zergliederungskunst hier beschreiben, jeden Knochen, Knorpel, Muskel, jede Membrane, jedes Ligament u. s. f. untersuchen wollte. Dieses Werk hätte sich leicht um einen ganzen Band vermehren lassen, wenn man in diese Materie tiefer hätte eindringen, und so viele physiologische und anatomische Schriften ausschreiben wollen. Von dem ganzen Spiele des Ein- und Ausathmens, das der erste Grund zur Sprache ist, hat uns der unsterbliche Haller einen ganzen Band in 4°. hinterlassen. (*) Wenn die Frage ist, wie die

Violine

(*) Albert v. Hallers Anfangsgründe der Physiologie des menschlichen Körpers 3ter Band. Das Athemholen, die Stimme.

CHAPTER 3: On the organs of speech

57

Chapter 3

On the organs of speech and their function

§ 26

It would be going too far were one to examine anatomically every organ that Nature employs for human speech, every bone, cartilage, muscle, every membrane, every ligament, and so forth. If one were to penetrate this material deeper, and evaluate so many physiological and anatomical writings, this part of our work could expand into a whole volume. On the topic of breathing in and out, which is the starting point of speech, the immortal Haller has bequeathed us an entire quarto volume.(*) If the question is, how

(*) Albert von Haller's "Anfangsgründe der Physiologie des menschlichen Körpers." 3rd Volume, Breathing and Speech.

[1] recte: Albrecht von Haller (1708–1777)
[2] Berlin 1766

161

Figure 2. Page 57 of the "Mechanism" in the original typesetting (German version) on the left, the same page in the commented version translated into English.

6 Observations and Curiosities

During our intensive analysis of the "Mechanismus" we came across some facts that seem remarkable to us.

6.1 Speech production

First of all, Kempelen's sober view on speech production is remarkable. Although he was not the first to deal on an empirical basis with this topic, his consistency and frankness is as astonishing as his illustrations that almost always are striking and witty. For instance he explains how voiced plosives anatomically could be articulated in a similar way to that done in the 20th century [10]. His illustrations are perfect examples not only of his skill in etching copper plates but also of his ingenuity of finding catchy examples (Fig. 3). To explain the physiological processes of articulating voiced plosives Kempelen asks the reader to imagine a recorder that is inserted into a pig's bladder except for the mouthpiece. Blowing into the recorder a sound will be heard as long as the air pressure inside the bladder is not equal to the air pressure outside of it.

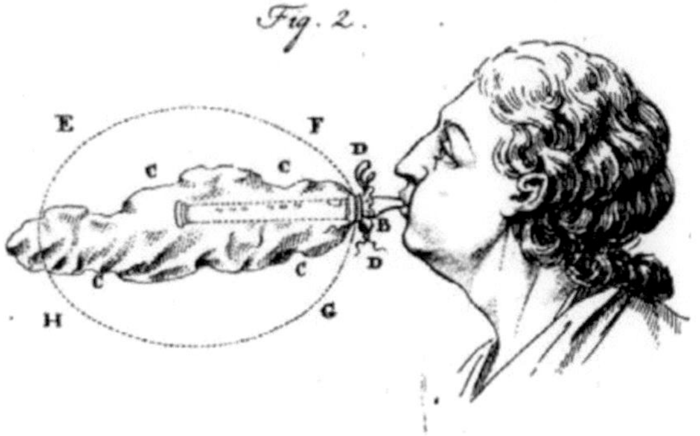

Figure 3. Figure 2 of Kempelen's Table XI showing the illustrative model of the articulation of voiced plosives.

Regardless of Kempelen's often brilliant explanatory approaches there are some passages of his book that are hard to understand even for linguists with experience in reading archaic German. This sporadically may display Kempelen's own uncertainty of some aspects but is mostly due to a use of language that is very different from the one today. Besides grammatical constructions that are unusual from a modern perspective, several words had then a more or less different meaning and/or connotation than they do today.

6.2 Extra-linguistic knowledge

For the understanding of some specific ideas "extra-linguistic" knowledge is needed. For instance Kempelen compares the German umlaut vowels (ä, ö, ü) to the "semitones of the piano". To understand this (striking) analogy one has firstly to know that alterations of musical notes in German are named with a suffix added to the stem note (i. e. "C#" is called "Cis"). Secondly umlaut letters in black letter originally were written by putting a small "e" on top of the "stem letter". So an umlaut vowel is "extended" similarly to an altered musical note.

Comparing the book with respect to its diction and orthography with Kempelen's letters and notes, it is hard to believe that all these originate from the same author. The "Mechanismus" often makes an almost modern impression in his spelling and diction while Kempelen's letters are typical examples of the "blurred" diction of the 18th century. In fact the text of Kempelen's book seems to be revised by the publisher to some extent. This is due to the language reform that was performed in Austria around 1780 based on the ideas of Johann Christoph Gottsched.

6.3 Book subscribers

Kempelen's book was published by *praenumeration*. At the beginning of the book a list of subscribers is given: 122 by name and 73 "unnamed subscribers". In the advertisement for the praenumeration it is explicitly said that copies will be printed only for the subscribers [9].[5] Amongst the named subscribers we could find names like the later Tsar Paul I of Russia and his wife, the archduchess Maria Christina of Austria, and her husband, and many other nobles and magnates. We find also several private scholars but almost no scholars that are well known today. Nevertheless we know of some, such as Georg Christoph Lichtenberg, Justus Christian Loder and Gottlieb von Windisch, who owned a copy of Kempelen's book. Also the dedicatee of the "Mechanismus", Ignaz von Born, is not listed. His portrait is shown on the frontispiece of the book (often this illustration being erroneously taken as that of Kempelen) with a Latin dedication meaning "His and nature's friend, Ignaz von Born – the author". Ignaz von Born died very shortly after the publication. It is not known why Kempelen dedicated his book to Born. The copper-plate engraving used for the frontispiece was not made by Kempelen but comes from Johann (or Joseph) Georg Mansfeld following a miniature by Heinrich Friedrich Füger. Born had commissioned this miniature shortly before his death, and then sent copies of the engraving to various persons, including Kempelen.

6.4 Copper plates

The remaining 26 copper plates were made by Kempelen himself. In general they show a fine understanding of the engraving technique. Nonetheless for some of the figures Kempelen seems to have had trouble with the correct representation of the third dimension. Also some of the representations seem to have been made with less care than others (e.g. the depiction of his organ-like prototype on Tab. XVII). Neither the mechanics of the keys nor the bellows could have worked as shown there. Kempelen's depiction of the "mouth" of the final version of his speaking machine is peculiar as well. It is shown in three tables (Tab. XXIII–XXV) in the original versions, see Fig. 4 here. Its cross-section, from representation to representation, assumes an increasingly curved form, while its dimensions remain the same.

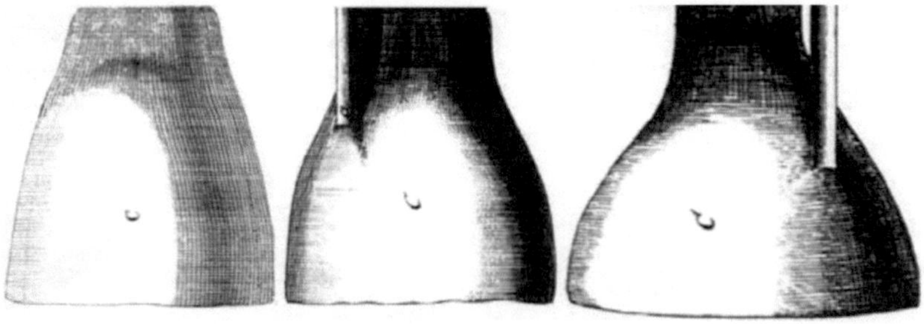

Figure 4. Kempelen's depiction of the speaking machine's mouth-funnel on tables XXIII, XXIV and XXV of the "Mechanismus" (from left to right).[6]

[5] Due to similar but better documented cases of praenumeration it is very likely that some of the subscribers purchased more than one copy.

[6] Experiments with replicas of the speaking machine made by the first author show that the exact shape of the mouth funnel is less relevant for the sound quality.

6.5 Phonetic alphabet

Kempelen's attempt to develop a kind of phonetic alphabet on the base of the established set of characters of the German alphabet inevitably failed from a modern point of view. An example is the assignment of the letter <I> to the German vowels [i] and [ɪ] but also to the consonants [j] and [ʝ] (as allophones of /j/ as in *Jagd*). The letter <J> could then be used to represent the sound [ʒ]. In French this sound is in fact represented by exactly this letter, but in the other languages that Kempelen treats, it is not. On the other hand, he associates the voiceless counterpart [ʃ] with the orthographic representation <SCH>, which in turn is a unique feature of German. This mixture of different orthographic and phonetic notations often causes some confusion for today's readers who have a background in phonetic transcription. Nevertheless, it must be borne in mind that the first clear-cut separation of graphemes and phonemes was achieved only by the Prague school in the 1920s. It is clear from Kempelen's formulations that he was well aware of the problematic nature of his approach, but apparently adopted it for practical reasons rather than introducing an abstract and purely phonetic-based alphabet.

7 Errors

There are few serious mistakes in Kempelen's book. Besides a number of typographical errors, that could not attributed to him but to the typesetter, there are also some content-related mistakes. The two most relevant occur as part of one line of argumentation and were taken over from the same reference. In chapter 2 Kempelen argues that language was not given by God but invented by humans and that there was no *Urlanguage* from which derives every existing language. To demonstrate this he compares the numerals 1 to 10 from twelve very different languages "of peoples who live far from each other and could not have had any knowledge of each other". If these languages derived from one single *Urlanguage* there should be fundamental similarities in their basic vocabulary such as numerals.

He presents the numerals for Korean and "Formosan" but also for Hungarian, Turkish and Khoisan languages. His source was the "Oriental and Occidental A, B, C-Book" by Benjamin Schulze from 1769 [11]. The examples given by Schulze [11] are predominantly accurate for most languages, although the pseudo-phonetic transcription sometimes has marked defects which certainly make identification of the evidence difficult at times. For the Korean number examples a curious mistake occurred: the separate native Korean and Sino-Korean numbers were mixed to a single "doubled" one.

A particularly amusing case is the fallacy that relates to "Formosan" that snared Schulze [11], and by inheritance Kempelen. Fritz & Schulze clearly used as their source the fraudulent work "An Historical and Geographical Description of Formosa, an Island Subject to the Emperor of Japan" written by a certain George Psalmanazar in 1704 [12]. Unfortunately Psalmanazar had no knowledge of the land that he described including the language. The examples of the Formosan language, like everything else in the book, were a pure invention and have nothing in common with actual Austronesian Formosan languages.

8 Conclusion

Kempelen's "Mechanismus der menschlichen Sprache" was a milestone of early phonetics and remains famous today. Besides the pioneering content of the book, its style of writing is often enthralling and entertaining in the best sense of the word. Though it was conceptualized for a different purpose it can be considered as a textbook for basic elements of linguistics.

When we decided to make a new, transliterated and translated edition of Kempelen's book that could be usable as well as useful for many researchers, we were aware that we would have to solve various types of problems. But we had not expected the great diversity of challenges that finally arose. First of all various editorial questions had to be solved in a way that makes the text easily readable but also keeps as much meta-information present in the book as possible. And in regards to content we found several difficulties. Some passages are hard to understand. And even if the fundamental line of argument is obvious it sometimes can be very challenging to explain it in other words or to translate it faithfully into another language.

Kempelen's disclosure of the construction of his speaking machine was not entirely voluntary. He felt compelled to do so to keep the critical voices silent. But nonetheless the "Mechanismus" and especially its fifth chapter on the speaking machine can be seen as an early form of open source publication: The operating principle was disclosed to a degree that allows a fundamental analysis of this approach. This is a clear difference from contemporaneous approaches like, e.g., that of Christian Gottlieb Kratzenstein, who published only a very vague description of his "vowel organ" that is hardly sufficient for a precise reproduction.

In addition, when one has dealt intensively with Kempelen's book one comes across a multitude of secondary aspects that nonetheless throw a light on the conditions of its origin and thus help to improve its understanding.

References

[1] LICHTENBERG, G. CHR.: *Nachricht von der Sprachmaschine des Herrn Hofr. von Kempelen*. In: *Magazin für das Neueste aus Physik und Naturgeschichte*, vol. 8, part 1, pp. 84-102, 1791.

[2] UNGER, J. K.: *Wolfgang von Kempelen. Nekrolog, Zeitschrift von und für Ungern, zur Beförderung der vaterländischen Geschichte, Erdkunde und Litteratur*. vol. 5, no. 5, pp. 313–317, 1804.

[3] KEMPELEN, W.V., *Wolfgangs von Kempelen k. k. wirklichen Hofraths Mechanismus der menschlichen Sprache nebst Beschreibung seiner sprechenden Maschine*. Edited by Herbert E. Brekle & Wolfgang Wildgen. Bad Cannstatt: Fromman, 1970.

[4] KEMPELEN, W.V., *Wolfgang von Kempelen: Mechanismus der menschlichen Sprache / The Mechanism of Human Speech. Kommentierte Transliteration & Übersetzung ins Englische / Commented transliteration & translation into English*. Edited by Fabian Brackhane, Richard Sproat & Jürgen Trouvain. Dresden: TUDpress, in press.

[5] REININGER, A., *Wolfgang von Kempelen – Eine Biografie*. Wien: Praesens, 2007.

[6] REININGER, A., *Wolfgang von Kempelen. A Biography*. Translated from German by Peter Waugh. East European Monographs distributed by Columbia University Press, 2012.

[7] RM., *Windisch, K. G. v.: Briefe über den Schachspieler des Hrn. von Kempelen: Review. Allgemeine deutsche Bibliothek*. vol. 58, no. 1, pp. 275-280, 1783.

[8] SPROAT, R., *Language, Technology, and Society*. Oxford University Press, Oxford, 2010.

[9] KRAUS, P. *Ankündigung eines Werks unter dem Titel: Wolfgangs von Kempelen k. k. wirklichen Hofraths bey der k. Hungarischen und Siebenbürgischen Hofkanzley. Mechanismus der menschlichen Sprache; nebst der Beschreibung seiner sprechenden Maschine, Intelligenzblatt der Allgemeinen Literatur-Zeitung*, no. 17, 3 Februar, 1790. pp. 129-132.

[10] OHALA, J. and RIORDAN, C. J., *Passive vocal tract enlargement during voiced stops. Speech Communication Papers*, 1979, p. 89.

[11] SCHULZE, B.: *Orientalisch- und occidentalisches A.B.C-Buch welches hundert Alphabethe nebst ihrer Aussprache so bey den meisten Europäisch-Asiatisch-Africanisch- und Americanischen Völkern und Nationen gebräuchlich sind.* Naumburg, Zeiss, 1769.

[12] PSALMANAZAR, G.: *An Historical and Geographical Description of Formosa, an Island Subject to the Emperor of Japan.* London: Brown, 1704.

Kempelen's speaking machine: Experiences with replicas

Fabian Brackhane [1], Mária Gósy [2]

[1] *Institut für Deutsche Sprache (Mannheim), Germany,*
[2] *Research Institute for Linguistics, Hungarian Academy of Sciences (Budapest), Hungary*
brackhane@ids-mannheim.de

Abstract: There are a number of recent replicas of Wolfgang von Kempelen's speaking machine. Although all of them are explicitly based on Kempelen's own description nearly none of them are identical in construction and sound. In this paper we want to illustrate some of these differences and their reasons for five replicas built by ourselves.

1 Introduction

Wolfgang von Kempelen's speaking machine presumably is the most famous, but certainly the most important early approach to create artificial speech. Apart from its strong reference to human anatomy this is also due to the fact that the construction had been extensively described in his also popular book "Mechanismus der menschlichen Sprache" (1791) [1].

Based on Kempelen's description very early replicas have been made. The first one we know of dates around 1797 [2]. But the fascination with this device remains until today. Exemplarily from 1967 to the present day at least 11 replicas have been made by various researchers (see section 1.1.3). Interestingly, despite Kempelen's description of building the machine in his book nearly no one is like the other. This can be explained by various reasons including the facts that there are some parts of the machine that (i) lack the detailed information and (ii) are not clearly described and/or illustrated in Kempelen's own book, such as the missing information about the outer structure and material of the machine or the vague description of the reed pipe.

The goal of this paper is to discuss some constructional details of five 21st century replicas compared to those of the original machine as described in [1]. We want to highlight the constructional consequences of some insufficient information of Kempelen's own description. In addition, we will present some acoustic characteristics of the replicas' sounding that could be a basis for further research of the replicas. Similarities and differences in the constructing processes could help to better understand the strengths and weaknesses of these replicas of a 226-year old mechanical speaking machine. For space reasons, we focus on the representations of four organs of articulation, such as lungs, glottis, nose and mouth and, additionally, on the creation of fricative and trill sounds. We will show that (i) all replicas have more similarities than differences, and (ii) their 'child voice', as was described in Kempelen's era, can be proved by acoustic analysis.

1.1 Sources about the speaking machine

There are mainly two sources that give us reliable information about the construction of Kempelen's approach to speech synthesis. Firstly, the reports of Carl Friedrich Hindenburg [3] and Johann Jacob Ebert [4], which are strongly related to each other and therefore could be counted as a single source. Secondly, of course, Kempelen's own description in [1].

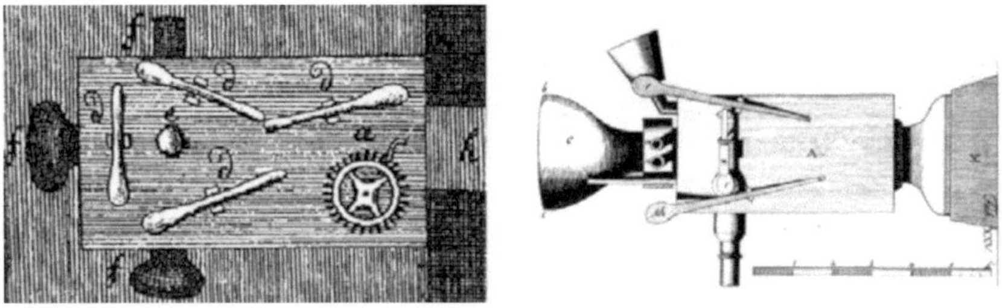

Figure 1a+b. Top views of the windchest of Kempelen's speaking machine in [3] (left) and [1] (right). On the left side: The mouth funnel, on the right: The connection to the bellows. On the top of the windchest: Several controllers for the generation of fricatives and pitch modification.

1.1.1 Hindenburg & Ebert

Hindenburg's and Ebert's publications are strongly related to each other.[1] They described an early version of the speaking machine presented to the public in 1784 during Kempelen's journey through Europe presenting his "Mechanical chess player". Both descriptions are rather short and partly hard to understand. Obviously neither Hindenburg nor Ebert had the opportunity to fully understand the operating principle of the machine. Nonetheless it is obvious that the device both authors had seen was very similar to the one described in [1] but seems to have been much more complex in its controlling (see Fig. 1).

1.1.2 Kempelen's "Mechanismus"[2]

Kempelen devoted the whole final fifth chapter of his book to his speaking machine and the history of its development. The description of the construction covers 42 pages with 9 additional scaled copper plates engraved by himself. At first glance this description seems to be very detailed and precise. However, if one wants to replicate the speaking machine based only on this information he becomes aware of many missing details. Some of these can be read off the drawings that do indeed show a high level of accuracy. Although Kempelen was known as a gifted illustrator and engraver some of his copper plates show shortcomings especially representing tree-dimensional objects. Additionally, the "Mechanismus" seemingly describes no existing device but a more or less idealized (and reduced?) version.

From these sources it is not entirely clear what the speaking machine in its final form looked like. In the Deutsches Museum, Munich there is a speaking machine that at least seems to originate from Kempelen to a large extent. It has been copied conscientiously and shows more similarity to the descriptions of Hindenburg and Ebert in [3; 4] than to Kempelen's own in [1].[3]

1.1.3 Replicas

A whole range of replicas has been made in the second half of the 20th and early 21th century (Table 1). Unfortunately only for some of them descriptions were published which furthermore mostly are not very detailed. For pictures of most of these replicas see [5].

---

[1] Both were published by the same publisher within a year. Additionally, Ebert refers to Hindenburg's book and replicates partly his illustration of the speaking machine.

[2] Full title: "Wolfgangs von Kempelen k. k. wirklichen Hofraths Mechanismus der menschlichen Sprache nebst der Beschreibung seiner sprechenden Maschine. Mit XXVII Kupfertafeln." (Wolfgang von Kempelen Imperial-royal Court Councillor's Mechanism of Human Speech along with the Description of his Speaking Machine. With 27 Copper Plates.)

[3] For licensing reasons it is not possible to give a picture of this device here.

Table 1. Modern replicas of Kempelen's speaking machine (following [5: 103]). Rerefences are given if possible.

Label	Year	Builder	Location	Features[4]	Reference
	1967	van den Broeke	Utrecht	2	[6]
	1968	Liénard	Paris	1	[7]
	1993	Howard	York	3	p. m.[5]
1	2000	Nikléczy & Olaszy	Budapest	1	[8]
	2001	Durin	Montluçon	2	p. m.[6]
	2004	Felderer, Strouhal & Scheid	Vienna	4	[9]
2	2007	Brackhane, Bauer & Mayer	Saarbrücken	2	
	2008	Durin	Montluçon	2	p. m.[5]
3_a	2009	Brackhane & Mayer	Dresden	2	
3_b	2009	Brackhane & Mayer	Paderborn	2	
4	2017	Brackhane & Mayer	Mannheim	2	

Despite the fact that Kempelen's device for creating artificial speech was not fully successful and at least is somewhat inconvenient, his speaking machine is a fascinating approach for understanding speech production by simulating speech by one's own hands. Although nearly all of the speech organ representations show deviations from the human body, it was nonetheless the first approach to speech synthesis that takes the human anatomy seriously into account. Reading Kempelen's description it is hard to imagine that this device could have anything in common with human speech.

On the other hand, the construction seems to be simple enough to just try it out of curiosity. Although one comes across many difficulties during the building process, the fascination grows side by side. In addition, the motivation of enhancing parts of the replica and/or trying different solutions leads to a more or less continuous work on this topic, and could shed light on further knowledge about some important nuances (odds and ends) of human articulation. Kempelen's machine could be regarded as the predecessor of the present-day 'articulatory synthesizers' from several aspects.

All of the replicas basically rely on [1]. Nonetheless nearly none of them are identical but show changes in various details and various extend of their construction. In the following paragraphs we will explain the deviations in the construction of our five replicas compared to Kempelen's description as well as the reasons of the deviations (Fig. 2). The speaking machine consists of three major parts which we will discuss separately: The outer structure (panel, box and bellows frame), windchest, and bellows.

2 Analyzed replicas

The five replicas we intended to compare are the followings: 1. replica developed in Budapest (called "replica 1" hereafter), 2. four replicas developed in Saarbrücken for several institutions ("replicas 2, 3_{a+b} and 4").

[4] 1 = faithful replica, 2 = with minor changes, that do not affect the functionality, 3 = with major changes, that partly affect the functionality and design, 4 = modern adaption

[5] Personal message by David Howard.

[6] Personal message by Jean Jeltsch

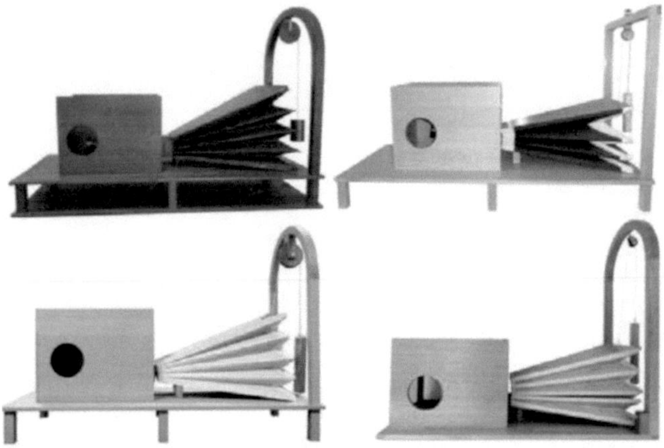

Figure 2. The replica models reported here: 1 (top left), 2 (top right), 3_{a+b} (bottom left) and 4 (bottom right). The framework of 1 is intended to be very close to that of Kempelen's original machine while replicas 2–4 show miscellaneous changes in constructional details.

The replica at Budapest ("replica 1") was initiated by two phoneticians, Péter Nikléczy and Gábor Olaszy of the Phonetics Department of the Research Institute for Linguistics. The main reason for building the machine was to participate in the Exhibition for the Millennium of the Hungarian State in 2000. In addition, researchers wanted to get an impression of the acoustics of Kempelen's original machine.

In 2007, the first author made a replica on the occasion of the 16th ICPhS congress in Saarbrücken ("replica 2"). This was on initiative of Jürgen Trouvain who has organized an accompanying exhibition on the history of phonetic sciences. Due to the complexity of the project the local organ building firm of Hugo Mayer (Heusweiler/Saar) was asked to support us with manpower and knowledge. The organ builder finally sponsored us by building the entire outer structure such as bellows, the foundation and the outer chest. Due to time constraints constructional compromises had to be made for the construction of some components such as the windchest and the reed pipe. These temporarily deviations will be illustrated too in the following sections.

In 2009, the first author was asked to build two identical replicas for the Technical University of Dresden and the Heinz Nixdorf MuseumsForum, Paderborn ("replicas 3_{a+b}"). It was decided to continue cooperation with the organ builder for these replicas as well as for replica 4 made in 2017 for the Institut für Deutsche Sprache, Mannheim ("replica 4"). For these three replicas ("3_{a+b}+4") the organ builder was responsible for the outer parts, the bellows and the blanks of the windchests and the reed pipes.

Replica 1 was intended to be an exact implementation of Kempelen's description. In contrast, replicas 2–4 were built according to pragmatic aspects. The overall constructional principle of [1] was retained, but we also wanted to be able to easily take the replicas apart for demonstration and (experimental) changes. So, some constructional aspects were adjusted to this aim. Replicas 2 and 4 were to be used for experiments and research and therefore conceptualized as constant work in progress (see also [10; 11]).

2.1 The outer structure

There are almost no details on the construction of the outer structures of these replicas. Such information is given by Kempelen neither about the material nor the dimensions. Only the proportions can be deduced from his scaled figures. As a consequence, the analyzed replicas show differences in this respect.

For replica 1, the outer structure, like all wooden parts, was made of teakwood. This kind of wood was judged to be the most appropriate one among the available hardwoods of the time. For replica 2, varnished spruce wood was used for cost reasons while for replicas 3_{a+b} and 4 these parts were made of waxed oak wood which is a very robust material and represents a high quality. The entire outer structure of replica 4 was defined in order to be able to dismantled and transported easily in a compact package.

The panel on which all parts of the machine (except the windchest) are fixed was made by Kempelen in such a way that it contained two separate boards connected by six wooden bases. This was likely to compensate the low height of the tables at Kempelen's time (see replica in Fig. 2 top left, the speaking machine is generally operated by a person standing at the machine). For replicas 2 and 3, we omitted the (second) bottom panel but retained the six wooden bases in each case (see Fig. 2, top right and bottom left). For replica 4, these bases were omitted, as well (see Fig. 2 bottom right).

The wooden box that encloses the windchest has no functional purpose. It just covers the windchest for protection. In addition, Kempelen obviously did not want his audience to see how the machine was operated. The measurements of the boxes for all four replicas were taken from the specimen in the Deutsches Museum.

Nowadays, it is important that the audience should be able to see how speech is simulated. Although its cover is movable, the box turned out to be a hindrance presenting the replicas. For this reason, the box of replica 4 was made partially of acrylic glass (side parts in the front and on the right). In addition, the parts of the box were not glued but only put together with wooden dowels. So, a dismantling and space-saving transportation is possible.

2.2 Windchest

The windchest of replica 1 was made again of teakwood. The upper side is not glued but can be twisted off, so the internal parts can be shown with some effort.

For the first prototype of replica 2, laminated wood was chosen for cost reasons. In addition, this windchest was made with an inner volume one and a half times of Kempelen's measures in order to have enough space in the windchest for making changes of some components. As it turned out this enlarged dimensions caused resonance vibrations and therefore damped the vibration of the reed pipe. So, another windchest with the original inner dimension was made after having found the right working constructions for all inner parts. This time we used nut wood following the specimen in the Deutsches Museum.

For replicas 3_{a+b} and 4, material and dimensions of the windchest were maintained. However, for the last one the wooden top was replaced by acrylic glass so that the audience could see what is happening inside the windchest during operation.

2.3 Levers for fricatives

If the windchest is made following Kempelen's specifications it becomes difficult to arrange the controlling levers for the valves of the fricative generators. They easily get into conflict with the "nostrils" if these are arranged too straddled (if they are arranged too narrow, this results in operating problems, too). For the connection between the levers and the valves, Kempelen speaks of "thin wire".

Therefore brass wire was used for replicas 2 and 3. But it turned out that wire (of course) is not flexible enough to compensate for even very small inaccuracies in the arrangement of levers, valves and the corresponding drilling in the top of the windchest. For this reason, the wire was replaced by nylon thread for replicas 2 and 4. The developers of replica 1 chose a specific textile thread that is usually used by shoemakers when sewing shoes.

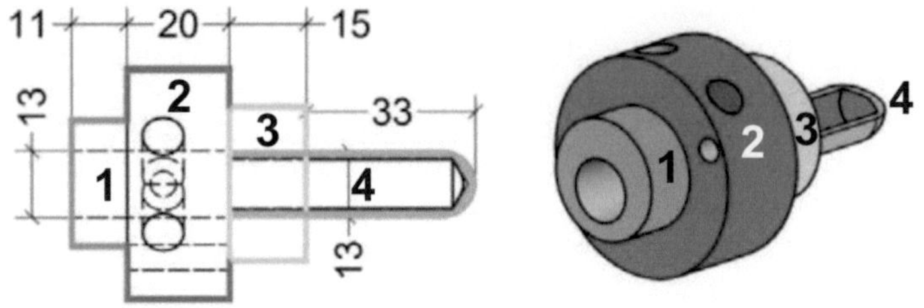

Figure 3. Sectional drawing (left) and perspective illustration (right) of the *reed pipe* for replicas 3_{a+b} and 4. 1: Connection piece to the mouth funnel, 2: The 'nostril' segment, 3: *Block* of the reed pipe, 4: *Shallot* of the reed pipe (colored version online). © Orgelbau Mayer 2017

2.4 Device for /r/-sounds

While replica 1 is equipped for simulating trill sounds following Kempelen's description, replicas 2–4 do not contain a specific "r"-device. The reason for this difference is mainly language-specific meaning that replica 1 is used particularly for simulating Hungarian speech while the other replicas are used mainly for German utterances. Since in German the phoneme /r/, in contrast to Hungarian, can be represented in most cases by the vocalic allophone /ɐ/ or at least by a very weak fricative /ʁ/, there was no imperative to build this rather delicate part into the machine. Kempelen admits that the machine is best in producing utterances in French and Italian (which both require consonantal /r/-sounds) while German speech is more difficult to produce than the ones mentioned previously [1: 455].

2.5 Reed pipe

2.5.1 Beating reeds

Kempelen's representation of the human glottis is closely based on so called *reed pipes* with *beating reeds* as used in pipe organs (which have an operating principle similar to a clarinet, see Fig. 3). Kempelen's *reed pipe*, however, differs from typical organ *reed pipes* in some constructive aspects. The reason for this is unknown but according to [1] Kempelen had no deeper knowledge of organ building.

Replica 1 firstly was equipped with a *reed pipe* made as close as possible to the requirements in [1]. Because of their unsatisfactory functionality after a year of trials a second one was made with slight modifications.

For replica 2, in the beginning a modern *reed pipe* was used that was not made for this purpose (and did not follow Kempelen's specifications) but was made from lead and brass instead of wood and also had slightly different proportions. In 2008, this could be replaced by a wooden one close to Kempelen's drawings. However, also in this case it was impossible to make the *reed pipe* following exactly the drawing on Kempelen's Tab. XVIII: The conic drilling of the *block* as shown there is nearly impossible to make if the *reed pipe* is made from one single piece of wood as demanded by Kempelen. For this reason it was decided to make a cylindrical drilling that of course had to have the same inner diameter as the height of the *shallot*.

For replicas 3_{a+b} and 4, the organ builder developed a completely new solution containing a loose wooden *shallot* that is clamped in the cylindrical drilling of the wooden *block* (Fig. 3). In every case we made the *block* of the *reed pipe* and the segment of the nostrils from one piece of wood, deviating from Kempelen's specifications. Just putting the nose segment on the *block* resulted in a constant instability.

Kempelen chose ivory as material for the pipe's *reed*. This is very unusual and has no model in organ building. Ivory is not very flexible but brittle and therefore hard to thin out.

Figure 4. The *free reed* pipe for replica 2. While the nostril segment and the block of the proper *reed pipe* are retained (mid), the shallot is replaced by an adapter that contains a *free reed* from a *reed organ* (right). On the left: The mouth funnel.

For every five replicas, very thin ivory coats of piano keys were polished and used. Kempelen's information about the *reed's* thickness ("like a playing card" [1: 411]) is not helpful. In fact, the thickness had to be explored empirically. Here, it is necessary not to thin out the *reed* too much to preserve some degree of tension.For replica 1 it is about 0.2 mm, for re plicas 2–4 it ranges from 0.25 to 0.4 mm. Also, it is very helpful to get some curvature at the top of the *reed*. Otherwise it will work unreliably and only with very low air pressure. The leathering of the *reed's* bottom (as demanded by Kempelen) significantly hampers its vibration. For this reason the *reed* of replica 1 is not leathered.

2.5.2 Free reed

Almost simultaneously to Kempelen's work Christian Gottlieb Kratzenstein had worked on a "vowel organ" that did at least produce the vowels *a*, *e*, *i*, *o*, *u* [12]. In contrast to Kempelen, Kratzenstein's theory on vowel articulation and speech production in general was very defective. Although he also used a reed pipe for simulating the human glottis, his supposed findings on human anatomy led him to the development of a variant of reed pipes, the *free reed*. With this construction the *reed* does not rest on the top of a *shallot* but it is mounted in a frame where it can freely oscillate.

These *reeds* are distinguished by a very smooth sound without noise components, but in contrast to beating reeds no variation of pitch by increasing or decreasing air pressure is possible. However, in order to experimentally combine Kempelen's and Kratzenstein's approach, the first author build a *free reed* for replica 2. Manufacturing of a free reed pipe has to be even more precise than for a beating reed. For this reason, we reused a free reed from a reed organ and combined it with a custom-made groove (Fig. 4). The sound of the speaking machine using this free reed was smooth as expected but because of its absolute monotony it was less authentic than using *beating reeds*.

2.6 Bellows

Kempelen gave no exact description concerning the construction, measurements or material of the bellows. It seems that it was obvious for him that the bellows should be made like traditional organ bellows, just smaller. Their size can be derived from proportions on Tab. XXII in [1] to some degree. The bellows of all five replicas are 40 cm in length and 26/11 cm in width (v-shaped), respectively.

However, we know about the bellows design and its number of direct folds. It is a classical *wedge-bellows* with four *direct folds*. For replica 1, following Kempelen's depiction four folds were adjusted. For replica 2, the organ builder made only three folds for financial reasons which results in a very tight air reservoir. As a consequence replicas 3_{a+b} and 4 got bellows with four folds.

There is also no exact definition of the construction and material of the valves. We made *not-return valves* as in traditional organ bellows.

2.7 Mouth funnel

For the funnel representing the mouth Kempelen again chose a very unusual material. He describes it as the upper part of a bottle made from natural rubber. Since these bottles were not produced any longer we had to think about another material and thought of casting it in rubber. So, for replica 1, a specific rubber object was made by a professional rubber worker according to Kempelen's figures.

Due to time constraints in 2007, a mug made from rubber was used for replica 2 (Fig. 4, left). The bottom was cut off and the rubber was rolled into the right dimensions. Although this was considered as a temporary solution it had proven itself so well that replicas 3_{a+b} were also equipped with funnels like this. Apart from aesthetic aspects these rubber funnels have the danger of leakage in itself if they are not made very carefully. For replica 4, this sort of funnel was replaced by a tailor-made version made by 3d printing. The flexible plastic available is completely sufficient for our purposes.

The inner diameter of the mouth funnel seems to be around 45 mm on Kempelen's drawings. This part was slightly enlarged to 55–60 mm being more comfortable to use. This variation seems to have no influence on the sound.

3 Fundamental frequency and spectra based on speech of replicas

Kempelen's information on the dimensions of the reed pipe (that is absolutely crucial for the speaking machine) is very vague (cf. section 3.4). Therefore, it is not surprising that the voice qualities of all the replicas are somehow different. However, they all have in common that they sound as the voice of a child, caused by a relatively high fundamental frequency of the produced speech. This phenomenon was described by Kempelen himself as a useful feature to conceal the machine's deficits, such as the lack of fricatives and articulatory disfluencies [1: 442].[7]

The factors causing the voice quality characteristic of a child are primarily the proportions and thickness of the ivory reed (cf. section 3.4). The different dimensions of the diverse reeds cause differences in the mean fundamental frequency of the replicas reported here. Replica 1 has a pitch of ca. 350 Hz while that of replica 2 is ca. 250 Hz (for both reed pipes). The fundamental frequency of replicas 3_{a+b} and 4 is about 500 Hz and 400 Hz respectively.

Considerable differences can also be seen in the spectrograms and spectra when comparing them (Fig. 5). The faithful reed pipe of replica 2 shows a more complex spectrum than replica 1 but it contains more noise components and less differentiated distribution of energy at the same time. For replica 4 the reed's very high fundamental frequency results in a spectrographic depiction that differs significantly from the others and resembles the spectrograms taken of very young children who have high fundamental frequency in their speech.[8] All three replicas analyzed here show an energy maximum around 1,700 Hz. Replica 1 has an additional energy maximum around 1,100 Hz.

4 Discussion

Kempelen's speaking machine unquestionably is an important keystone for the development of mechanical approaches to speech synthesis that has preserved its fascination until today. Motivated by his seemingly detailed description in [1] a considerable number of replicas have been made during the last 50 years. In this paper, we have described and partly compared five of them made by ourselves.

---

[7] Also many contemporary correspondents reported a similar sound quality [2: 154; 3: 51; 4: 51].

[8] The reed of one specimen of replica 3 shows a very similar spectrogram.

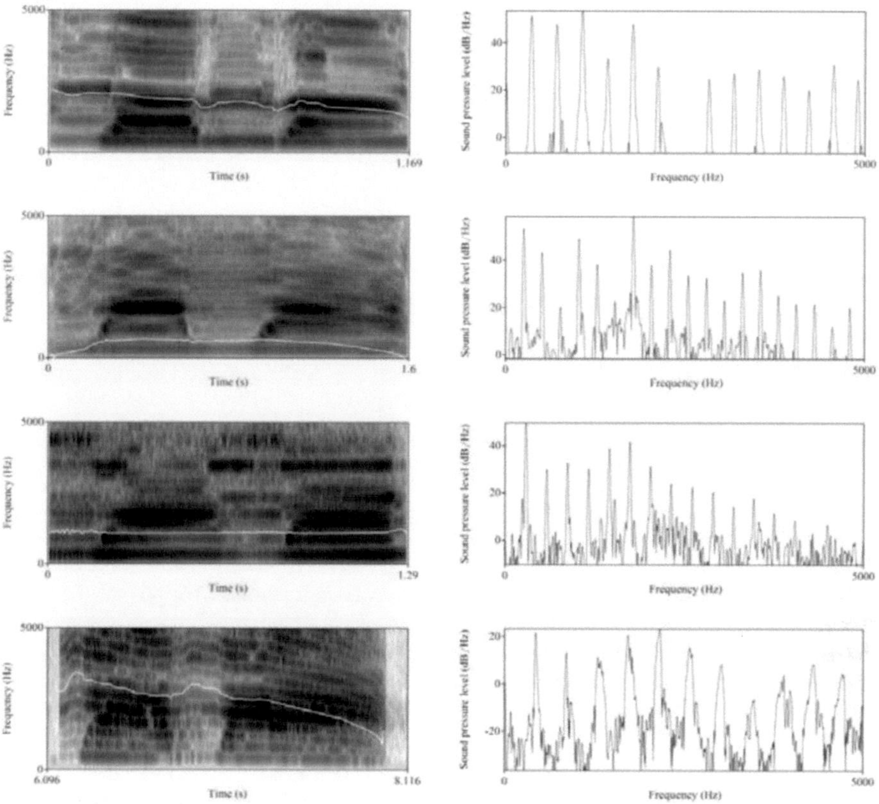

Figure 5. Spectrograms and pitch contours for the utterance /'mama'/ (left) and short-term spectra from 0 to 5 kHz of the stressed (first) vowel (right) for the replica 1, replica 2 with beating reed, replica 2 with free reed and replica 4 (from top to bottom).

Although Kempelen's own detailed description is a solid foundation for building replicas, information is missing for a large amount of details that are of vital importance. Their exact construction could only be investigated by trial and error. This leads to several constructional differences of the replicas reported here. Additional differences are due to different intentions from which the replicas were made: True copies following Kempelen's description in every detail versus modified replications, which are adjusted to their intended usage for research and teaching. So, we can conclude that the replicas show great similarity in their general design but they have noticeable differences in constructional details, and as a consequence, they show differences in their acoustic results.

Our acoustic analysis proved that all of our replicas produce speech in a way that shows strong similarities in quality to the speech production of a child. But the construction of the *reed pipe* – the representation of the human glottis – is much more difficult than Kempelen's description suggests. Different approaches to implement the requirements as well as to achieve a reliable functionality caused differences in the synthesis quality of the replicas. However, all of them share a similar high fundamental frequency when producing speech. Each replica is a close and high quality imitation of the machine built 226 years ago demonstrating various solutions for several constructional challenges. There is no question on a competition among the replicas. They provide a very useful opportunity to be able to look at a mechanic construction and functioning of the human speech organs with the 21st knowledge of human articulation.

Further acoustic and perceptual research of all the replicas' speech will show various interrelations between constructions and sounding. For this, an examination of more different replicas than the five presented here is desirable for a more comprehensive impression.

5 Acknowledgements

Thanks to Annette Klepp for improving the English version of this paper and to M.S. for always having great ideas.

References

[1] KEMPELEN, W.: Wolfgangs von Kempelen k. k. wirklichen Hofraths Mechanismus der menschlichen Sprache nebst Beschreibung seiner sprechenden Maschine. Degen, Vienna, 1791.

[2] GOETHE, J. W.: Goethes Werke, herausgegeben im Auftrage der Großherzogin Sophie von Sachsen. IV. Abtheilung, 12. Band, p. 154, 1893.

[3] HINDENBURG, C. F.: Ueber den Schachspieler des Herrn von Kempelen – nebst einer Beschreibung seiner Sprachmaschine. Müller, Leipzig, 1784.

[4] EBERT, J. J.: Nachricht von dem berühmten Schachspieler und der Sprachmaschine des K. K. Hofkammerraths Herrn von Kempelen. Müller, Leipzig, 1785.

[5] BRACKHANE, F.: Die Sprechmaschine Wolfgang von Kempelens – Von den Originalen bis zu den Nachbauten. In: W. BARRY & J. TROUVAIN (eds.): Phonus 16, pp. 49–148, 2011.

[6] VAN DEN BROEKE, M.: *Wolfgang von Kempelen's speaking machine as a performer.* In: van den Broeke, M., van Heuven, V. and Zonneveld, W.: *Studies for Antoine Cohen.* Foris Publications, Dordrecht, 1983.

[7] LIENARD, J.-S.: *From speaking machines to speech synthesis*. Proc. 12th ICPhS Aix-en-Provence, 1991. Vol. 1, 18-27.

[8] NIKLÉCZY, P., OLASZY, G.: Kempelen's speaking machine from 1791: possibilities and limitations (Recovering a 200-year-old technology). In: Grazer Linguistische Studien 62, 111–120, 2004.

[9] FELDERER, B., STROUHAL, E.: *Kempelen – zwei Maschinen.* Sonderzahl, Wien, 2004.

[10] TROUVAIN, J., BRACKHANE, F.: Wolfgang von Kempelen's "speaking machine" as an instrument for demonstration and research. In: Proc. 17th International Congress of Phonetic Sciences, Hong Kong, pp. 164-167.

[11] TROUVAIN, J., BRACKHANE, F.: The Relevance Today of Wolfgang von Kempelen's "Speaking Machine". In: *PHONUS* 16, pp. 149-166.

[12] KRATZENSTEIN, CHR. G.: Tentamen resolvendi problema. Petersburg 1781. Übersetzt und kommentiert von Christian Korpiun. TUDpress, Dresden, 2016.

The Sennheiser Vocoder Goes Digital – On a German R&D Project in the 1970s

Rüdiger Hoffmann[1], *Gritta Gramm*[2]

[1]*Technische Universität Dresden, Institut für Akustik und Sprachkommunikation**
[2]*Sennheiser Heritage Archives, Sennheiser electronic GmbH & Co.KG, Wedemark*
ruediger.hoffmann@tu-dresden.de

Abstract: In the history of speech technology, the vocoder plays the role of a "guiding fossil", which introduced the ways to speech analysis and synthesis with electronic means. The general approach is continuously important in contemporary communication systems, but now with digital implementations. This paper describes a research project of Sennheiser electronic from the 1970s, which gives an impressive example for the transition from the classical analog systems to digital, computer-based solutions.

1 Introduction

Any electronic device which is able to analyze the speech signal, to produce a parametric description of it, and to re-synthesize the speech signal from these parameters (Figure 1), is called a *Vocoder* (voice encoder and decoder) following a proposal of HOMER DUDLEY (1896–1980), who constructed the first prototype in the U.S. in the 1930s. The first intended application was in speech transmission, because the transfer of the coded signal requires essentially less bandwidth than that of the original signal.

The first vocoders were so-called *channel vocoders*, where the parametrization of the speech signal is performed by measuring and transferring the signal power in a number of adjacent frequency bands (channels). The information whether the signal is voiced or unvoiced and, if voiced, the fundamental frequency (for the prosody or "speech melody") must be transferred as additional parameters.

Because the development of the vocoder required extensive research in speech analysis as well as in speech synthesis, it is regarded as the "guiding fossil" of the whole electronic speech technology (and also of electronic music). However, it is hard to reveal the history of the early vocoders, because they produced coded speech, which could be utilized for secure communication channels mainly in military applications. The most prominent example is DUDLEY's Vocoder, which was adapted as part of the SIGSALY system ("Project X") of the Bell Laboratories [8], which was used in World War II and after. Documents which could tell the worldwide history of the vocoder have therefore been kept secret for a long time and are partially lost.

This paper describes a facet of the vocoder development in Germany using a set of research reports and related documents, which are stored in the Heritage Center of the company Sennheiser electronic at Wedemark, Germany, and have been declassified meanwhile. Unless otherwise noted, the contents are based on this collection. The main purpose is to demonstrate the step from the analog to the digital vocoder implementation, which was feasible due to the progress of computer engineering in the 1970s.

*The research project was partially supported by the German BMBF, grant number 01UQ1601A.

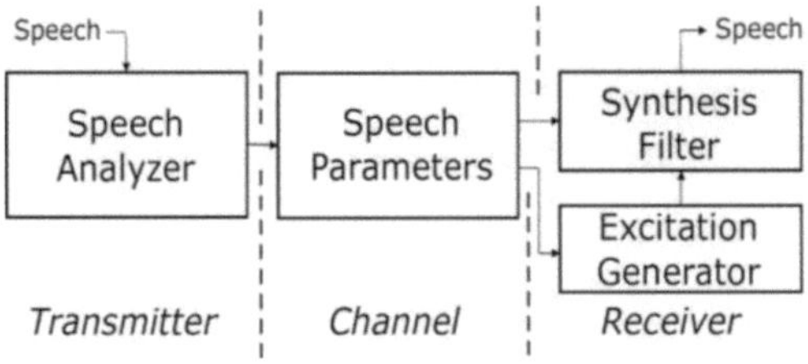

Figure 1. Basic principle of a vocoder-like system for speech compression and transmission [17].

2 The vocoder in Germany

Due to war destruction and secrecy problems, it is hard to reconstruct the early history of the vocoder in Germany. It is obvious, that there was a vocoder-like patent of the German engineer KARL-OTTO SCHMIDT (1901–1981) in 1932 [27], five years earlier than the respective patent of DUDLEY [6]. SCHMIDT was with the *Reichspostzentralamt* Berlin since 1931. His doctoral thesis was supervised by KARL WILLY WAGNER (1883–1953), the founder of the *Heinrich-Hertz-Institut* (HHI) in Berlin. The work of WAGNER in speech research influenced the ideas of DUDLEY on his vocoder [38, p. 48]. In 1937, the *Forschungsanstalt der Deutschen Reichspost* was founded in Kleinmachnow near Berlin [7, 25][1], where SCHMIDT worked until the end of WW II. The well-known author of several textbooks in radio engineering, FRITZ VILBIG (1903–1988), was appointed deputy director of the *Forschungsanstalt*. Two decades later, he was the co-author of a comprehensive overview on the development of speech compression systems [39].

Generally, wide-band communication via cables was one of the research fields of the *Forschungsanstalt* [25]. However, only few documents are left in the archives, and there is no evidence that SCHMIDT really implemented a device which was analogous to the vocoder [18]. Nevertheless, there is some probability for this. SCHMIDT, who continued to publish about bandwidth problems [28, 29], summarized on frequency compression in 1967: "The most important and best known invention in this field is the vocoder. [...] It has a predecessor, which is 7 years older" [30]. This can be interpreted as a concealed pointer to a real device.

The *Deutsche Reichspost* was also one of the initiators, when the aforesaid *Heinrich-Hertz-Institut* was founded in Berlin [15]. This institute played an important role in the development of acoustics and communication. In the founding year 1928, the engineer OSKAR VIERLING (1904–1986) changed to this institute as assistant of the director K. W. WAGNER. VIERLING was a leading scientist in audio engineering and electronic music [5, 40]. He was appointed lecturer (1938) and extraordinary professor (1944) at the TH Hannover. During the war, he headed a secret laboratory in Ebermannstadt, which was specially erected for this purpose as "Burg Feuerstein" in 1941. Among other topics, systems for the encryption of speech were investigated there [37].

It is reported that the company Siemens was involved in this development, cooperating with the HHI as well as with VIERLING's laboratory. MANFRED SCHROEDER (1926–2009), who was an international expert in vocoder technology [32], supposed that Siemens had vocoder-like systems before the end of the war [38, p. 190–191]. It is also said that fragments of a vocoder have been found in a Bavarian lake in 1999 [38, p. 194].

Evidently, Siemens was involved in the optimization of the bandwidth requirements in

[1] The *Forschungsanstalt der Deutschen Reichspost* owned a subbranch with the similarly sounding name *Forschungsstelle der Deutschen Reichspost*, which secretly supervised communication channels during the war. Headed by the engineer KURT VETTERLEIN, the deciphering of the transatlantic telephone traffic of the Allies, which was secured by the A-3 system of the Bell Laboratories [8, p. 292 ff.], was achieved there [12, 24].

speech transmission since the 1930s. FELIX STRECKER (1891–1951), who was a collaborator of RICHARD FELDTKELLER at the Siemens company in that time [11], described a vocoder-like system in a conference paper from 1935 [36].

A real fixed-point after so much speculation appears in 1955, when the Siemens company made a hitherto unknown prototype of a vocoder available for the development of electronic music. This vocoder got famous in the history of electronic sound production, before it was given to the *Deutsches Museum* Munich in 1994 [26, 35].

A research prototype of the channel vocoder was also developed in the eastern part of Germany in the framework of a thesis at the TH Dresden [22]. The project initiated the research in speech technology at the later TU Dresden, but it was never included in encryption tasks.

While the production of cryptographic devices was not allowed in Germany in the years after WW II, several developments started in the 1950s. A first official department for encryption solutions was founded in 1950 as part of the Foreign Ministry ("Referat 114"). It was closed in 1956, when the *Zentralstelle für Chiffrierwesen* (ZfCH) was founded in Bonn-Mehlem [2, p. II/293].

In the 1960s, the systems for the different kinds of secure transmission tasks were summarized to the ELCRO family, which consisted of the product groups ELCROVOX, ELCROTEL, ELCROBIT, ELCRODAT, and ELCROMUX [2]. Among the ELCRO family, the ELCROVOX series aimed to secure voice communication. The development and manufacturing was originally assigned to the companies Siemens and Telefunken. The corresponding division of Telefunken was later renamed to ANT [4]. The series was started with ELCROVOX 1/0 in 1966. This system was a combination of an encryption device SB 490 and a vocoder VOC 490, the latter being delivered by Sennheiser electronic (Figure 2). It was mainly used for secure communication between the German Foreign Office and the embassies until the late 1970s. According to [23], ELCROVOX 1/0 was a replica of an American system, consisting of the encryption device KG-13 and the vocoder HY-2 (from Bell Labs), which had been introduced in 1961. More about the American system can be found in [38, pp. 170–173].

Besides, ELCROVOX 1 was applied for military purposes in the *NATO Narrow Band Secure Voice System* (NBSV-I) [2, p. I/243]. Among the different developments in this series, ELCROVOX 1/3 should be mentioned because it plays a role in the project F 600, which will be described later. The piece in the collections of the Museum for Communication Frankfurt (Figure 3) was produced in 1972.

3 Sennheiser electronic and the vocoder

The personal life of Prof. Dr. FRITZ SENNHEISER (1912–2010), the founder of Sennheiser electronic, shows early connecting points with the history of the vocoder. When he studied Electrical Engineering at the *Technische Hochschule* Berlin, he used the chance to work at the *Heinrich-Hertz-Institut*, where he labored with OSKAR VIERLING in the field of speech and electronic music. When VIERLING changed to the TH Hannover in 1938, SENNHEISER followed him, received the doctorate under his supervision, and replaced him in the lectures, when he stayed at *Burg Feuerstein* [5, 34].

The institute was transferred from Hannover to the village Wennebostel after a bombing attack in 1943. Immediately after the war, at June 1, 1945, FRITZ SENNHEISER founded here his "Laboratory W" (with W for Wennebostel, today part of the parish Wedemark).

The cooperation of VIERLING and SENNHEISER started with electronic music, but during the war, they worked in the field of encryption. There is no detailed information about this, because the material at *Burg Feuerstein* as well as in the institute in Wennebostel was confiscated by the Allies. Nevertheless, the existing scientific contacts yielded cooperation with

Figure 2. The vocoder VOC 490 as part of the encryption system ELCROVOX 1/0. Photographs of an exhibit of the Museum for Communication Frankfurt, reproduced with permission. Left: complete device, front plate removed. Right: one of the channel filters with the Sennheiser logo at the small transformer.

Figure 3. The encryption system ELCROVOX 1/3 of the Museum for Communication Frankfurt. Left: Overall view [23], © Museumsstiftung Post und Telekommunikation. Right: Partial view on the interior, showing the 18-channel vocoder system (probably called VNA 1) with two boards (melody analysis / transmitter channels 1–3) partially pulled out; reproduced with permission.

many partners in the post-war times, which resulted in an involvement of Laboratory W in the development of vocoders [34, p. 23].

An anecdote tells, that SENNHEISER's laboratory was involved in the installation of the secure communication, when the German chancellor ADENAUER visited Moscow in 1955. There, the beginning of diplomatic relations was declared, and the Soviet government promised the return of the German prisoners of war. The equipment was situated in the special train of the delegation, where four officers served for the secure communication [20, 21].

Laboratory W was renamed to "Sennheiser electronic" in 1958. In the following years, Sennheiser electronic started the production of the VOC 490, a channel vocoder with 18 channels (Figure 2). It was applied as part of the aforementioned ELCROVOX 1/0, which was introduced in 1966.

According to the materials in the archives, a first notice of HANS-JOACHIM GRIESE about a *Vocoder for high noise levels* emerged in October 1965. This invention was patented 1968 [13]. FRITZ SENNHEISER valued Dr. GRIESE, who was also a scholar of VIERLING, as "the most creative collaborator of that time" [34, p. 255].

In the 1970s, Sennheiser electronic was engaged in research projects concerning the vocoder, which will be explained in the following section. However, the company finished all activities for the application of vocoders in encryption systems in 1977. It was apparently desired, to summarize the experiences from many years of production of analog channel vocoders, resulting in the design of the VOC 493. A complete documentation in the archives of the company tells that VOC 493 is designed as a part of a speech encryption system. The vocoder consists of 14 printed circuit boards in European format (100×160 mm^2), a tub-like wiring and a board with two balancing transformers. The spectral range covers 200 Hz ... 6500 Hz and is subdivided into 18 channels. The melody range is 77 Hz ... 500 Hz. One data frame needs 49 bits. However, we do not know whether this final design was ever applied in a real system of the ELCROVOX series.

4 The R&D projects of the 1970s

4.1 Participation in the project F 600

At the end of 1970 or in the beginning of 1971, FRITZ SENNHEISER was informed about a project idea, concerning the development of an improved vocoder with minimized bit rate. While the existing encryption system ELCROVOX 1/3 worked at 1800 bit/s, the new system should cope with a bit rate of 600 ... 1000 bit/s, whereas the speech quality should not be worse than that of the existing system. The project was called "Frequenzkompressor 600", where "600" indicated the ultimate goal for the bit rate. It was subdivided to three project partners and started in the middle of 1971. The results are summarized in four research reports, dated from December, 1971, to June, 1973.

It was the project part of Sennheiser electronic, to reduce especially the bit rate of the melody code. As already mentioned, the melody extraction is the most complicated task when designing a channel vocoder. The Sennheiser vocoder VOC 490 used originally a method which was internally called "analog melody", which applied a controlled, slanted lowpass filter for the extraction of the fundamental frequency. Another method, called "digital melody", counted the time between two zero crossings of the pitch signal by means of quartz generated pulses. These methods are summarized in the monograph of W. HESS [16]. Because the "digital melody" led to more reliable measurements, it was introduced in practice. Apparently, existing VOC 490 systems were upgraded with the new method and were then called VOC 490A. One of the devices in the collection of the Museum for Communication in Frankfurt [23] is provided with a notice that the upgrade was performed in 1973. The museum owns a separate switching unit, which allows the connection of the encryption unit SB 490 with either VOC 490 or VOC 490A. A later channel vocoder system, which was similar to VNA 1, but equipped with "digital melody", was called VOC 491.

A vocoder of even this type was used by the Sennheiser team to optimize the melody analysis in the F 600 project. Most important, the experiments moved partially to a digital computer. A computer of the type ERA GA 18/30 from General Automation was installed at Sennheiser electronic at the end of 1971. This type of computers was compatible to the *IBM 1800 Data Acquisition and Control System* (DACS), a typical early process controller which was equipped with D/A and A/D converters [19]. The availability of this computer enabled to investigate software solutions for digital filters, cepstrum and LPC methods and others. The programs, normally written in Fortran IV, were far from real time, but encouraged the developers to concentrate to the goal of a fully digital vocoder.

4.2 SK 1 – the digital vocoder

With the start of the second half-year 1973, Sennheiser electronic was granted with a new project "Simulation of a new channel vocoder", abbreviated as SK 1. It aimed to a detailed investigation of a digital implementation. The computer ERA GA 18/30 continued to be used. The results were collected in 10 research reports, the last of them appearing in March, 1977.

The first approach included the transfer of the classical vocoder structure into equivalent software. The receiver part was implemented not only in time domain by means of stored impulse responses of the filters, but also in frequency domain with a digital third filter bank, the channels of which were (in the medium range of the frequency scale) similar to the hitherto used mel filter bank. For the transmitter part, the spectral features of a VOC 491 system were calculated via FFT, but the melody features were still taken from the VOC 491 hardware. The results were more or less satisfactory, but a reliable software implementation of the melody analysis was still missing.

Because the complex FFT spectrum was available, experiments were started to transfer either the complex spectrum or suited speech parameters, which could be extracted from the spectrum. Following several other experiments, the 6th research report from December 1975 directs the focus to formant parameters.

This decision was heavily influenced by the results of a meeting in Stockholm at the KTH institute of GUNNAR FANT in 1974. Most likely, this information means that researchers from Sennheiser electronic took part in the international *Speech Communication Seminar*, which was held in the Royal Institute of Technology at April 1–3, 1974. According to the proceedings [9], leading experts of the vocoder technology had been among the speakers.

There were two reasons for switching to formant based principles. At first, it seemed unlikely that the limited speech quality of channel vocoders could be further improved. Secondly, this existing quality was achieved for broadband speech, but could not be maintained for narrowband (standard telephone) speech, which was required, however, according to the customer.

Clearly, the description of voiced speech by a set of formant frequencies and bandwidths offers a very effective parametrization. This was successfully utilized in early speech synthesizers mainly by GUNNAR FANT (1919–2009), who had developed the formant synthesizers OVE I (1953) and OVE II (1961) [10]. Therefore it seemed natural to apply a formant synthesizer as the receiver part of a vocoder. However, this solution required the extraction of the formant parameters at the transmitter part of the vocoder in real time, which was very complicated with classical analog components [31]. This situation changed rapidly with the introduction of digital processing, and a first approach of a computer-simulated formant vocoder was published as early as 1963 [3].

The software implementation of the formant vocoder in the framework of the project SK 1 was performed from 1975 to 1977 with growing quality of the synthesized speech. The final architecture is shown in Figure 4, which may be elucidated by the following details:

- The complete algorithm is based on the magnitude spectrum of a speech frame, which is calculated by FFT. It is also used for the signal/pause and the voiced/unvoiced decision; for the latter, the relation of the signal energies of the upper and lower bands, resp., is considered.
- For voiced frames, the magnitude spectrum is "harmonized", which means, that it is reduced to the harmonics of the pitch (the "melody frequency"). The pitch is estimated by analyzing the spectral periodicity. Adjacent spectral lines are merged by parabolic interpolation. If a line does not fit the harmonic structure, it is considered as a distortion.
- Three formant bands are selected from the harmonized spectrum. The estimation of the formant parameters (central frequency, bandwidth, amplitude) is basing on its modeling as a resonance curve.
- The treatment of unvoiced frames is similar to the channel vocoder, i. e., the energy in a number of frequency bands is calculated from the FFT spectrum.
- The receiver reconstructs the line spectrum from the formant information for voiced frames or from the channel information for unvoiced frames. For each line, a sinusoidal signal is provided, and all these signals are finally summarized. In the case of unvoiced frames, noise is introduced by a random conversion of the signs.

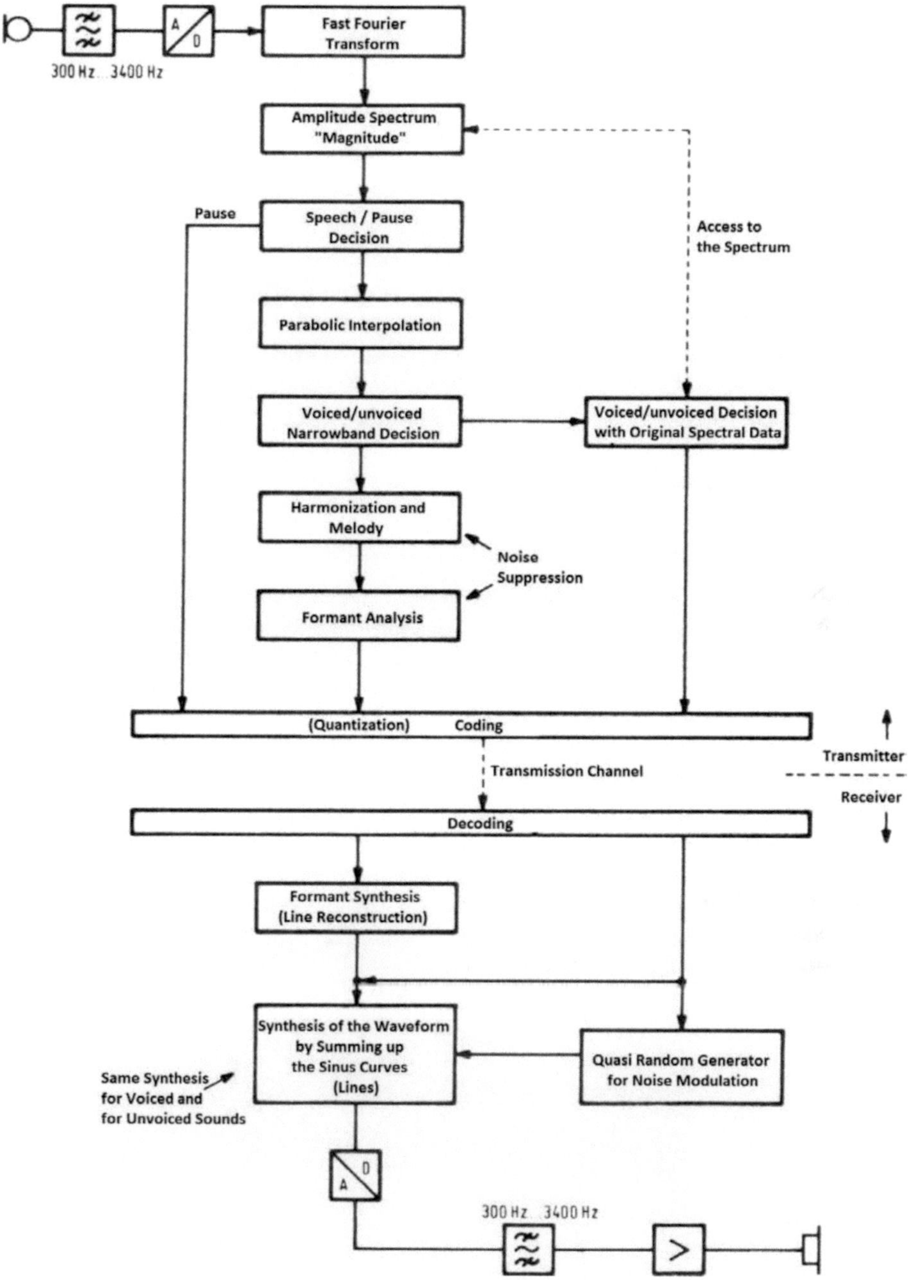

Figure 4. Flowgraph of the Sennheiser Minivocoder. Reproduction of the original graphics from the research report on the Minivocoder from 1977, except that the German inscriptions have been translated. The previous Sennheiser digital vocoder SK 1 followed the same software architecture, but the sampling frequency was twice as high. © Sennheiser electronic.

4.3 The Sennheiser "Minivocoder"

As already mentioned, the Sennheiser company finished the activities for the application of vocoders in encryption systems with the end of the SK 1 project. The experiences in digital vocoders had been saved for potential future applications as the "Minivocoder" in a research report, which is dated at the end of 1977. There were two essential differences compared to SK 1: the software was now running at the more modern, very popular process controller PDP 11, and the sampling rate was lowered from 16 kHz in SK 1 to 8 kHz, because the Minivocoder was intended to process narrowband speech (300 Hz ... 3400 Hz), which resulted in 128 samples per frame of 16 ms. Apart from this, the software architecture followed completely the structure of SK 1 (Figure 4).

The report is finished by an assessment of the computing expenses of the digital vocoder. The analysis of the developed software was performed for the worst (lowest) case of pitch, which was assumed to be 75 Hz. Then, a voiced frame required 103,901 operations, whereas an unvoiced frame needed only 44,783 operations. These numbers were too big for real time processing with the computers of that time, but the authors recognized the chance for a digital hardware solution, mainly due to the growing availability of special processors, which could perform the FFT very quickly.

5 VMS 201 – an application for entertainment

The commitment of the Sennheiser company in the vocoder technology had a final phase, in which the know-how was applied to the entertainment industry with allowance of the former contracting authority. A new "Sound Effect Vocoder" VSM 201 was presented at the 1977 conventions of the Audio Engineering Society in Paris and New York [1] and in a conference paper by H.-J. GRIESE and E. WERNER [14].

VSM 201 was a channel vocoder with 20 channels (100 Hz ... 8000 Hz), which could be manually controlled in several ways. The pitch extraction was omitted, because the excitation signal was typically introduced from external sources. The application was supported by the renowned film composer HEINZ FUNK (1915–2013), who not only sold the vocoder, but also used it in his music productions[2]. The device was listed in the catalogues of the company until 1981 [33]. Due to the pure analog construction, it showed a rather big number of control elements, which were not easy to handle, thus limiting the application to a small number of specialists in electronic music [34, p. 246].

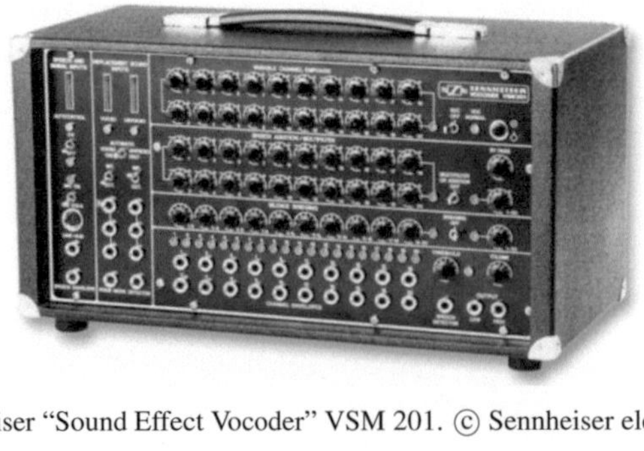

Figure 5. The Sennheiser "Sound Effect Vocoder" VSM 201. © Sennheiser electronic.

[2]A presentation of the VSM 201 combined with the MOOG synthesizer by HEINZ FUNK in a ZDF video clip from 1978 is available at YouTube: `https://www.youtube.com/watch?v=FLljyZ2ojbA` (verified May 05, 2017). FUNK also developed two demonstration tapes for the VSM 201; a copy of the second one from 1979 is preserved in the Sennheiser archives.

6 Conclusion and acknowledgements

Vocoders have a long history, ranging from the first attempts up to sophisticated solutions in voice codecs. Due to the proximity to secrecy applications, the history of vocoders has still numerous gaps. This work closes one of the gaps due to the availability of documents in the archives of Sennheiser electronics, which are analyzed here for the first time.

This paper gives rise to remember Prof. Dr. WOLFGANG NIEHOFF (1945–2013), who started his scientific career at the TU Dresden and came to Sennheiser electronic in 1988. After a talk at DAGA 2011 [18], he informed first author of the contributions of the Sennheiser company to vocoders and thus initiated the further investigation. Our cordial thanks go to Dr. ERHARD WERNER, who was involved in the vocoder projects as a young researcher. He readily supported our project and contributed numerous details from his personal memories. Furthermore, the authors thank Prof. Dr. JÖRG SENNHEISER for the permission and his kind support of the work.

Finally, we thank Mr. FRANK GNEGEL, head of the department "Collections" of the Museum for Communication in Frankfurt, and his team, who readily opened his resources to us and gave numerous explanations on early encryption devices, and Prof. Dr. KLAUS FELLBAUM (Berlin), who provided us with a historic magnetic tape with audio examples from vocoder experiments in the environment of the project F 600.

References

[1] AES Conventions, exhibitions of the Sennheiser vocoder VMS 201. *Journal of the Audio Engineering Society* 25 (1977), p. 68 (56th Convention, Paris), p. 616 (58th Convention, New York), p. 1050 (photograph of the demonstration by Sennheiser's HORST ANKERMANN).

[2] BECKH, J.: *Blitz & Anker. Informationstechnik – Geschichte, Hintergründe.* 2 vols. Norderstedt: BoD (2005).

[3] COKER, C. H.: *Computer-simulated analyzer for a formant vocoder.* Abstract, 66th Meeting of the Acoustical Society of America, in: *Journal of the Acoustical Society of America (JASA)* 35 (1963) 11, pp. 1911–1912.

[4] Crypto Museum, The Netherlands: Website, URL (19. 2. 2017): `www.cryptomuseum.com/`

[5] DONHAUSER, P.: *Elektrische Klangmaschinen. Die Pionierzeit in Deutschland und Österreich.* Wien, Köln, Weimar: Böhlau 2007.

[6] DUDLEY, H. W.: *Signaling System.* US Patent 2,098,956, patented Nov. 16, 1937.

[7] FAENSEN, H.: *Forschungsanstalt und Ministersitz: Was sich auf dem Gelände der Kleinmachnower Hakeburg ereignete.* In: *Post- und Telekommunikationsgeschichte* 3 (1997) 2, pp. 16–31.

[8] FAGEN, M. D. (ed.): *A history of engineering and science in the Bell system: national service in war and peace (1925–1975).* Bell Telephone Laboratories 1978. – Section on secure speech transmission: pp. 291–316.

[9] FANT, G. (ed.): *Speech Communication. Proceedings of the Speech Communication Seminar, Stockholm, April 1–3, 1974.* 4 volumes. Stockholm: Almqvist & Wiksell 1975.

[10] FANT, G.: *Half a century in phonetics and speech research.* Fonetik 2000, Swedish phonetics meeting in Skövde, May 24-26, 2000. URL (26. 3. 2017): `http://www.speech.kth.se/gunnarfant/halfcentury.pdf`

[11] FELDTKELLER, E.; GOETZELER, H. (eds.): *Pioniere der Wissenschaft bei Siemens.* Erlangen: Publicis MCD Verlag 1994.

[12] GELLERMANN, G. W.: *…und lauschten für Hitler. Geheime Reichssache: Die Abhörzentralen des Dritten Reiches.* Bonn: Bernard & Graefe 1991.

[13] GRIESE, H.-J.: *Vocoder für hohe Störlautstärken.* German patent 74/68, claimed 26. 1. 1967, patented 18. 9. 1968, unpublished.

[14] GRIESE, H. J.; WERNER, E.: *Vocoder techniques for synthetic and voice controlled sound generation.* In: *Journal of the Audio Engineering Society* 25 (1977), p. 50 (announcement), p. 318 (report), p. 340 (abstract). – Manuscript (in German) courtesy of E. WERNER.

[15] GUNDLACH, F. W.: *Das Heinrich-Hertz-Institut für Schwingungsforschung.* In: *50 Jahre Heinrich-Hertz-Institut.* Vortragsband, 18. und 19. Mai 1978, pp. 4–16.

[16] HESS, W.: *Pitch determination of speech signals–Algorithms and devices.* Berlin: Springer 1983.

[17] HOFFMANN, R.: *On the development of early vocoders.* In: *Proc. of the 2nd IEEE Conference on the History of Telecommunications (Histelcon).* Madrid, Nov. 3–5, 2010, pp. 359–364.

[18] HOFFMANN, R.: *Zur Entwicklung des Vocoders in Deutschland.* In: *DAGA 2011, 37. Jahrestagung für Akustik, Düsseldorf, March 21–24, 2011, Proceedings "Fortschritte der Akustik"*, pp. 149–150.

[19] IBM Archive: *Vintage views of products: IBM 1800.* URL (26. 3. 2017): `http://www-03.ibm.com/ibm/history/exhibits/vintage/vintage_4506VV4022.html`

[20] KILIAN, W.: *Adenauers Reise nach Moskau.* Freiburg: Herder 2005.

[21] Konrad-Adenauer-Stiftung, Website: *Zusammensetzung der Gesamtdelegation [von Adenauers Moskaureise 1955].* URL (3. 4. 2017):
`https://www.konrad-adenauer.de/download_file/force/1811`

[22] KROCKER, E.: *Aufbau und Untersuchung eines Übertragungssystems für synthetische Sprache.* In: *Wiss. Ztschr. TH Dresden* 6 (1956/57) 4, pp. 757–776.

[23] Museumsstiftung Post und Telekommunikation: Website Sammlungen, Objektdatenbank, URL (22. 2. 2017):
`http://sammlungen.museumsstiftung.de/kategorie/objektdatenbank/`

[24] PRÖSE, M.: *Chiffriermaschinen und Entzifferungsgeräte im Zweiten Weltkrieg.* München: Meidenbauer 2006.

[25] REUTER, M.: *100 Jahre technische Zentralämter der Post, 40 Jahre FTZ und PTZ in Darmstadt.* In: *Archiv für deutsche Postgeschichte* (1989) 1, pp. 5–17.

[26] SCHENK, S.: *Das Siemens-Studio für elektronische Musik. Geschichte, Technik und kompositorische Avantgarde um 1960.* Tutzing: Hans Schneider 2014 (Münchner Veröffentlichungen zur Musikgeschichte; 72).

[27] SCHMIDT, K.-O.: *Verfahren zur besseren Ausnutzung des Übertragungsweges.* German Patent 594 976, Feb. 27, 1932. — *Zusatzpatent.* German Patent 722 607, Jan. 14, 1939.

[28] SCHMIDT, K.-O.: *Frequenzbandbreite, Übermittlungszeit und Amplitudenstufenzahl (Geräuschabstand) bei den verschiedenen Nachrichtenarten im Rahmen der Shannon-Theorie.* In: *Fernmeldet. Ztschr.* 6 (1953) 12, pp. 555–563, and 7 (1954) 1, pp. 33–43.

[29] SCHMIDT, K.-O.: *Die Anforderungen synthetischer Sprache (Vocodersprache) und vorverformter Sprache an die Kanalkapazität des Übertragungsweges.* In: *NTZ* 14 (1961) 6, pp. 279–285.

[30] SCHMIDT, K.-O.; BROSZE, O.: *Fernsprech-Übertragung. Sprache – Sprachwandler – Sprachübertragung.* Berlin: Schiele & Schön 1967.

[31] SCHROEDER, M. R.: *Vocoders: analysis and synthesis of speech.* In: *Proceedings of the IEEE* 54 (1966) 5, pp. 720–734.

[32] SCHROEDER, M. R.: *Computer Speech – Recognition, Compression, Synthesis.* Berlin etc.: Springer 1999 (Springer Series in Information Sciences; 35).

[33] Sennheiser electronic: *Sound Effect Vocoder VSM 201.* In: *Sennheiser revue* 9 (ca. 1978), p. 117; 10 (1979), pp. 105–105; 11 (1981), p. 120.

[34] Sennheiser electronic: *60 Jahre Sennheiser – Die Chronik.* Wedemark 2005.

[35] Siemens Kulturprogramm: *Siemens-Studio für elektronische Musik.* München 1994.

[36] STRECKER, F.: *Nachrichtenfluss und Frequenzbandbreite.* In: *Veröffentlichungen aus dem Gebiete der Nachrichtentechnik*, vol. 5, no. 4, pp. 227–233, Berlin: Siemens & Halske 1935.

[37] THADEUSZ, F.: *Tarnname Schornsteinfeger.* In: *Der Spiegel* (2011) 16, pp. 121–122.

[38] TOMPKINS, D.: *How to wreck a nice beach: the vocoder from World War II to hip-hop.* Brooklyn: Melville House / Chicago: Stop Smiling Media 2010.

[39] VILBIG, F.; HAASE, K. H.: *Über einige Systeme zur Sprachbandkompression.* In: *Nachrichtentechnische Fachberichte, vol. 3 (Informationstheorie)*, pp. 81–92, Braunschweig: Vieweg 1956.

[40] VOIGT, W.: *Oskar Vierling, ein Wegbereiter der Elektroakustik für den Musikinstrumentenbau.* In: *Das Musikinstrument* 37 (1988), no. 1/2, pp. 214–221; no. 3/4, pp. 172–176.

Standard French vowel formants vs. characteristic tones of Rousselot: tuning forks technique reconsidered

Pavel A. Skrelin[1], *Ulyana E. Kochetkova*[1]

[1]*Saint Petersburg State University, Russia*
skrelin@phonetics.pu.ru, ukochetkova@phonetics.pu.ru

Abstract: In the current study the historical instrumental method of speech analysis using tuning forks is considered from a new point of view. The set of tuning forks for French oral vowels with the engraved frequency values described by Rousselot in the early 20th century is used in a number of experiments. Firstly, the frequencies of the tuning forks were measured with the use of modern methods of acoustic analysis. The accuracy of their values was proved, which allowed their comparison with modern data on French vowel formant frequencies. Eventually, the perception experiment was conducted to find out modern native speakers' perception strategies.

1 Introduction

The Department of Phonetics of the Saint Petersburg State University houses a wide collection of tuning forks and resonators. The head and founder of the department Lev Scherba studied in Paris and worked in the laboratory of Jean Pierre Rousselot (l'abbé Rousselot) in 1908 [3]. Thus Scherba was acquainted with the newest instrumental methods and techniques of that time. As he noted himself [28], he measured Russian vowels using Rousselot's tuning forks. In this relation a set of thirteen tuning forks adjusted to the French oral vowels from the Department collection deserves a special mention (see Fig.1). It was seemingly produced by E. Zimmermann, since the manufacturer's mark "E Z" is inscribed on the yoke of these forks. It means that the set could hardly be commissioned by Rousselot, as long as this scientist generally commissioned his instruments to R. Koenig [25, 31]. At the same time the values engraved on the tuning forks correspond precisely to the numerous descriptions of the French vowel characteristic tones by Rousselot [22, 25]. It makes us suppose that Scherba commissioned to Zimmermann this set composed according to Rousselot's data. The engraved values are in v.d., i.e. *vibrations doubles*, a French term which equals to the modern unit of Hertz. The set also includes a wooden hammer and a board with the inscribed symbols corresponding to the thirteen tuning forks.

Figure 1. The set of 13 tuning forks adjusted to the French oral vowels, Phonetic Department collection, Saint Petersburg State University, Russia (photo by the authors)

2 Background of the current study

Tuning forks are mostly known today for their use in music and in medicine. The fact of this dual usage can be observed from the beginning of their existence. A good example is a tuning fork invented and elaborated by English trumpet and lute player John Shore. When Shore played in Handel's orchestra, he gave one of his tuning forks to the composer. Then Handel gave it to the Foundling Hospital in 1751 [2]. Another field in which tuning forks traditionally serve as tools has always been physics and notably acoustics [1, 7, 31]. Therefore the tuning fork became one of the first devices of acoustic phonetics at the very beginning of the speech instrumental research [17, 18, 25].

2.1 Pitch tuning standards

In acoustics and, particularly, in experimental phonetics in 19th and in the early 20th century pitch was described by means of musical notation and/or physical terms. Musical notation was appropriate in cases when the tone was defined solely by ear. In numerous works of this period both notations are used [17, 18, 24]. However, the musical notation is sometimes misinterpreted because a variety of pitch tuning standards or systems existed at that time. It still exists today, although on a much smaller scale.

According to J. P. Rousselot [26], at the beginning of the 18th century the note “la” (or “A” in Latin nomenclature) consisted with 405 vibrations per second. Nevertheless, the orchestra tuned their instruments higher and higher in order to obtain brighter sound. Thus, there was a diversity of pitch tuning in Europe with maximum at 452.5 or even 455.5 vibrations per second. In Great Britain, as indicated in [2], 452 vibrations per second became a Philharmonic Pitch in 19th century. Another value, 435 vibrations per second at 18° C, was suggested by J. Lissajous. He was one of a group of French scientists and composers developing new pitch standard. This standard was adopted in France in 1859 [1] and announced as the International Pitch in 1885 [32]. In some sources this standard is also cited as the New Philarmonic Pitch [2]. The pitch which is most commonly applied nowadays to the so-called middle “la” is that of 440 vibrations per second known as the Stuttgart standard [1]. The initiator of its use is German amateur scientist J. H. Scheibler, who is also known as the tonometre inventor [31]. The advantage of this pitch standard is that it enables obtaining the whole number of vibrations for most of the notes [1, 26]. This pitch was used by Helmholtz in his “Physiological Theory of Music” [17]. This fact caused a misinterpretation of cited values when this work was translated into French and the musical notation was reffered to physical terms [26]. The pitch adopted by J. P. Rousselot in his studies differs from those mentioned above. It differs even from the French standard of his time because the investigator followed the system of Rudolf Koenig, whose instruments Rousselot employed [25, 31]. Koenig tuned his devices into the middle “ut” (i.e. “do” or “C”) at 256 vibrations per second at 20° C. Therefore the “la” was supposed to be at 426.6 [24]. This standard, only one octave higher, i.e. C at 512 Hz, is also known today for its clinical use and is named “scientific” or “philosophical” pitch [2]. This very pitch was applied by the tuning fork's inventor John Shore [2].

2.2 Physical terms diversity

There is a diversity of terms in most of relevant literature of the 19th century. Sometimes a number of them occur within the same work. As mentioned above, J. P. Rousselot calculates the values in *vibrations doubles*, i.e. “double” vibrations, the French term for vibrations per second. He sometimes translates them in a number of *vibrations simples* or *demi-vibrations*, i.e. a half of the “double” or “complete” vibration. The term *vibrations simples* was traditionally used in France [24, 25, 26, 27]. Outside France the widespread term was cycles per second (c.p.s. or c.s.) [1]. The unit of Hertz officially replaced it only in 1960 [6], although the name of Hertz was given to the unit in 1930. This discordance in terminology leads from time to time to some confusions even today. Thus the following equation shows the correspondence of various terms indicating the number of vibrations per second:

1 vibration per second = 1 v.d. (*vibration double*) = 2 v.s. (*vibrations simples*) = 2 d.v. (*demi-vibrations*) = 1 c.p.s. (cycle per second) = 1 Hz.

2.3 Measuring pitch with tuning forks: techniques used by J. P. Rousselot

Many different techniques to measure vowel pitch by means of tuning forks or resonators existed. One of them supposed setting the vocal tract as resonator for the tuning fork's sound. When the correct articulation for a concrete vowel was formed, the tuning fork should be placed nearby the mouth. Then it was struck not too strong in order to avoid too much additional noise. If the articulation was correct and the tuning fork's pitch was well found, the tuning fork's sound was reinforced [25]. Another technique intended the use of the weighted adjustable tuning fork (i. e. with sliders on its prongs). Once the sound enhancement was found, as in the previous case, it was possible to check the value through the lips position repetitive change. Rousselot gives an example of the sequence "á – ó – á – ó" etc. [26]. If the suggested value was correct, the last heard sound would be the target tone [26]. Rousselot also describes other two methods when a vowel was whispered or sung at a given note and then reinforced by a sounding tuning fork or a resonator [24, 25]. Although the last techniques were familiar to Rousselot, the suggested values of the French vowel characteristic tones (in v.d. or v.s.) apparently consisted with the first methods' result [22, 25]. Rousselot himself indicated in this relation that his whispered vowels differed from the silently articulated vowels and that singing vowels changed their characteristics [26].

2.4 French oral vowel system described by J. P. Rousselot

Rousselot gives a detailed description of the French vowel system including nasal vowels [22, 23, 25]. His definition of the front unrounded and back oral vowels is of special interest, since the characteristic tones of these vowels are represented in the set of the tuning forks. In the current study, Rousselot's terms and symbols are accompanied by the modern IPA notation.

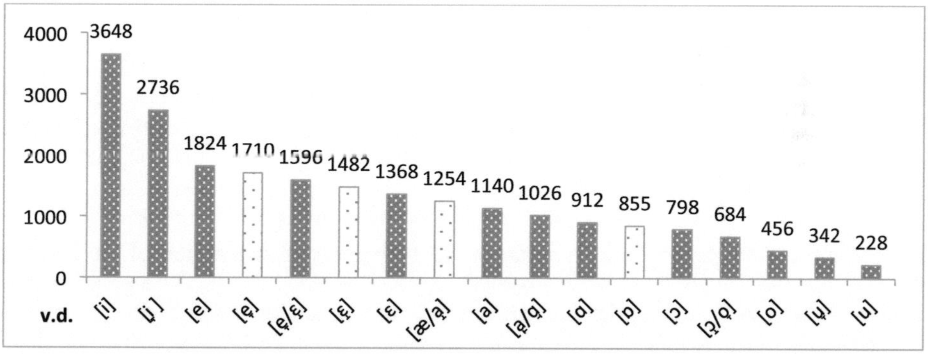

Figure 2. Characteristic tones frequency of the French oral vowels except [y], [ø], [œ] given by Rousselot in v.d. [22, 25] (values included in the set of tuning forks are given in dark grey; additional values are in white; 1v.d. = 1 Hz)

The description of French oral vowel system by Rousselot is more detailed than the modern classification (see Figure 2). He suggests two variants of the close vowels [i] and [u] (*i fermé* [i], *i moyen* [i̞]; *ou fermé* [u], *ou moyen* [u̞]) [22, 23]. Instead of the division into close-mid and open-mid vowels he gives three variants of the "mid" vowels for both rows. These are *e fermé* [e], *e moyen* [e̝/ɛ̝] and *e ouvert* [ɛ] of the front row and *o fermé* [o], *o moyen* [ɔ̝/o̞], *o ouvert* [ɔ] of the back row. He defines three variants of "a" in the same way. *A ouvert* corresponds to the front vowel [a], *a fermé* to the back vowel [ɑ] and *a moyen* [a̙/ɑ̘] to the modern term *a médiane*. The terms *fermé* ("close") and *ouvert* ("open") seemingly correspond to the modern standard French vowel nomenclature. Exceptions are the two "a" which are described in terms of aperture/ closeness by Rousselot. Nowadays traditional phonological descriptions use the terms of anteriority/ posteriority to define the corresponding vowels. It should also be noted that the term *fermé* , i.e. "close" (except the *a fermé*), is referred by Rousselot to the vowels in the word-final position or a stress-group-final position. The term *ouvert,* i.e. "open", indicates vowels mostly in a stressed syllable before [r] (the cases of e, a, o), as well as in other combinations with consonants [22]. The term *moyen* (i.e. "middle") corresponds mostly to unstressed allophones. In the latter case no difference is made by Rousselot between close-mid and open-mid vowels. Thus the unstressed variants of the [e] (*e* fermé) and [ɛ] (*e ouvert*) are considered together as [e̞/ɛ̝] (*e moyen*). In Rousselot's description, the term "middle" also represents the vowels in a stressed syllable before a certain consonant or a group of consonants. The number and quality of consonants is individual in each case [22, 23].

In some of his works [25] Rousselot gives additional values for several vowels (see white columns in the diagram, Fig.2). Three values represent *e moyen* and are indicated as [e̞], [e̞/ɛ̝], [ɛ̝]. Rounded "a°" [ɒ] corresponds to some regional variants of the back [ɑ]. The sound "a^ɛ" [æ/a̝] corresponds to the front vowel [a] in Parisian pronunciation. Thus, Rousselot tries to give a comprehensive and subtle description of French vowels' pronunciation which covers various regions. At the same time these additions are due to the author's ambition to elaborate a balanced vowel system. In his "Principles of Experimental Phonetics" [27] Rousselot assumes the existence of scales of vowel characteristic tones similar to those in music, although they differ in the number of elements and relationship within the scale. The main assumption of Rousselot [25, 27] is the existence of an equal intervallic span between two neighboring vowels (or their variants) which, ideally, should form a sort of scale. This idea can be in some way compared to the recent psychoacoustic scales of barks and ERBs. Nonetheless not all of the vowels fit in such a system correctly. Therefore some supplementary variants are suggested by Rousselot supposedly in order to help fill in the lacking cells of the assumed structure.

As it has already been mentioned, J. P. Rousselot gives precise values of the French vowel characteristic tones [22, 25]. As well as many of his predecessors [7, 17, 18], Rousselot tries to find one tone that gives the brightest resonance perceivable by ear. At the same time the author recognizes the existence of other characteristic frequencies, although they are weaker and seem to be less important for the vowel resonance perception [22, 25, 31]. Thus, Figure 2 represents only one characteristic tone value suggested by Rousselot [22, 25] in *vibrations doubles* (i.e. vibrations per second) for each oral vowel. Thirteen values correspond precisely to those engraved on the tuning forks in the collection. The four other meanings represent additional regional variants which are not included in the set of the tuning forks.

A comment has to be made in reference to individual pronunciation of the investigator and its relation to the cited values. Rousselot analyzes his students' and colleagues' pronunciation in relation to their geographical provenance and compares it to his own pronunciation [27]. Besides, when Rousselot presents the acoustic vowel description, he notes that "the mouth is adjusted to various vowels in the Haut-Angoumois region with the following notes" (translated by the authors) [22: 48]. It should be mentioned that the Haut-Angoumois region and notably Cellefrouin, the town Rousselot was from, is situated in the department of Charente in the south-west of France. The comparison of the characteristic tones of all the described variants allows us to conclude that Rousselot's main description of the French vowel system is based mostly on his own pronunciation [27]. Thus the set of the tuning forks from the Phonetic Department collection seemingly represents characteristics of Rousselot's own vowels. Consequently, it shows the Haut-Angoumois accent of the early 20th century.

2.5 Front rounded oral vowels as “composite” sounds

The absence of the front rounded vowels in the set of the tuning forks may be due to their "compound" (or "composite") nature, according to Rousselot [22, 25]. As shown in Table 1, the author gives two characteristic tones for these vowels. The first value corresponds to the front non-rounded vowel, the second value to the back vowel. Rousselot describes only the front rounded vowels and their variants by the two characteristic tones. Both tones belong to the more open vowels than the targets. Therefore [y] (*ü fermé*) in Rousselot’s system is composed by *i moyen* and *ou moyen* and not by *i fermé* and *ou fermé*, the same relation is observed for other vowels as well [22, 25].

Table 1. Characteristic tones of the French front rounded oral vowels according to Rousselot [22] (in v.d.; 1 v.d. = 1 Hz)

Rousselot's terms	IPA symbols	Rousselot's description	IPA symbols	Tone 1 (v.d.)	Tone 2 (v.d.)
ü fermé	[y]	i moyen + ou moyen	[u̞] + [i̞]	342	2736
ü moyen	[y̞]	e fermé + o fermé	[o] + [e]	456	1824
oe fermé	[ø]	e moyen + o moyen	[ɔ̝/o̞] + [e̞]	684	1710
oe moyen	[ø̞/œ̝]	e moyen + o ouvert	[ɔ] + [e̞/ɛ̝]	798	1596
oe ouvert	[œ]	e ouvert + a fermé	[ɑ] + [ɛ]	912	1368

3 Modern instrumental analysis data vs. Rousselot’s measurements

3.1 Evaluation of the tuning forks with modern methods of acoustic analysis

All 13 tuning forks of the described collection were recorded in the soundproof cabin. They were struck one by one by a special wooden hammer from the same set (see photo in Fig. 1). The instrumental analysis revealed the main fundamental frequency which in all cases was prevalent. A various number of additional frequencies were observed as well. Most of these frequencies had no correspondence to the main tuning fork’s tone. The appearance of such non-harmonic frequencies is commonly observed in otologists’ practice when tuning forks are struck off a metal or a wood [29].

The dominant tone emerges and can be heard in general after a short span of time after the beginning of the signal. A strong aperiodic noise appears when a tuning fork is struck. Then it gives place to the periodic dominant tone that lasts over 5 or even 7 seconds. The upper harmonic or non-harmonic periodic tones last as long as the fundamental tone or may fade 2 or 3 seconds after the initiation of the tuning fork. It corresponds to the data described in [19]. The middle of the dominant tone frequency band is calculated by means of the spectral analysis. The results show that the values engraved on the tuning forks are quite close to the frequencies calculated by modern methods of instrumental analysis. The difference from Rousselot’s values never overpasses one semitone. This fact allows us to appreciate the sophisticated ear technique used by Rousselot and to apply these values at the later stages of the study.

3.2 Formant value measurements using modern instrumental analysis

A comparison between modern and earlier data is of particular interest to the speech investigation history. Thus, the values engraved on the tuning forks which correspond to Rousselot’s description (see Figure 2) are put in parallel with a wide range of later instrumental data. These data contain formant characteristics of the French oral vowels measured from 1948 until

2012 [4, 5, 8, 9, 10, 11, 12, 14, 16, 21, 30, 33]. The juxtaposition (see Fig. 3) shows that the observations made by Rousselot in the early 20th century correspond to the F1 values quite rarely. This is the case of the back vowels [u], [o] or of their variants [u̟], [o̟/ɔ̟], [ɔ]. Such correspondence is less characteristic for [ɑ] and [a̟/ ɑ̟].

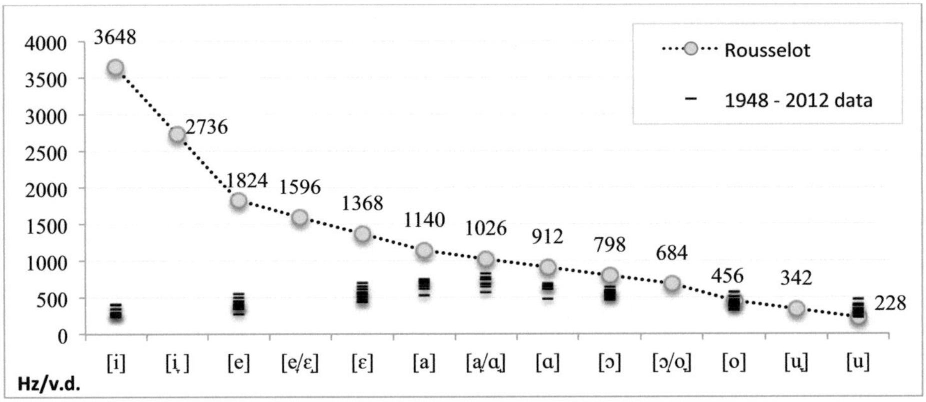

Figure 3. F1 of the French oral vowels except [y], [ø], [œ], data from 1948 until 2012, in Hz (isolated hyphen markers) vs. Rousselot's characteristic tones engraved on the tuning forks, in v.d. (continuous dotted line)

The last variant [a̟/ ɑ̟] can be related to the so-called "a" *médiane* measured by modern phoneticians. In our data this variant replaces the front [a] and the back [ɑ] from 1986 [4] onwards. Herewith formant characteristics of all vowels except [u] and [o] are lower than the corresponding characteristic tones calculated by Rousselot. It has to be mentioned that in modern pronunciation [u] and [o] appear to be more open than the corresponding vowels examined by Rousselot in the early 20th century. Among all vowel formants the most crucial mismatch with Rousselot's results is observed for the close vowel [i].

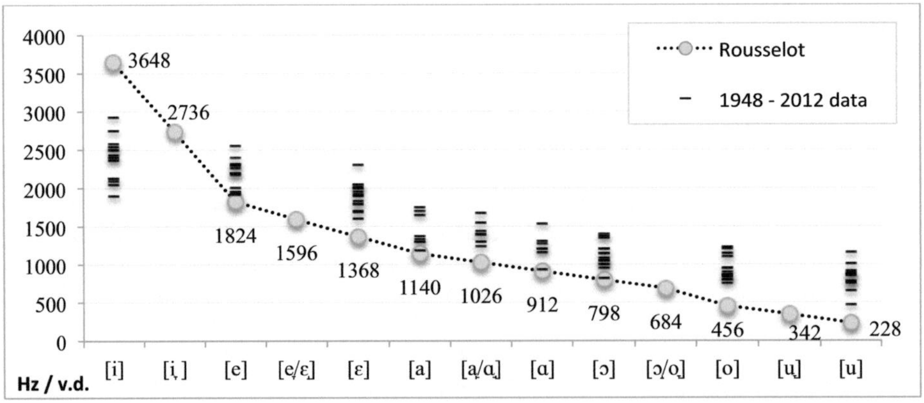

Figure 4. F2 of the French oral vowels except [y], [ø], [œ], data from 1948 until 2012, in Hz (isolated hyphen markers) vs. Rousselot's characteristic tones engraved on the tuning forks, in v.d. (continuous dotted line)

Contrary to the F1 data, F2 characteristics (see Figure 4) have greater data scattering. Nevertheless only [i] has a much higher value than the corresponding vowel second formant.

The tones of other vowels suggested by Rousselot are lower, especially those of [u] and [o]. Sometimes they coincide, as in cases of [e], [a], [ɑ], [ɔ]. The mismatches depend on the concrete corpus of the modern data. We can suppose that Rousselot perceived the second formant of the oral front unrounded and back vowels. The exception is provided by [o] and [u] (see above) and the characteristic tone of [i]. The latter value is close to the modern F3 frequency. Such closeness of the vowel characteristic tones evaluated by ear to the F2 values measured with modern instrumental analysis can be noticed from 1679 onwards [15]. This fact may be due to the psychoacoustic phenomenon of the better sensitivity of the human ear to high frequencies.

Figures 5 and 6 show conformity between the first characteristic tone given by Rousselot and the first formant value of [y]. The same relation is sometimes observed between the second formant of [ø] or [œ] and the corresponding tuning forks' tones. Although a variety of meaning is obvious, the difference between the modern and earlier data clearly appears in cases of the [œ] F1 value and the [y] F2 value. Only one individual meaning [14] is quite close to the F2 of [y]. The interesting fact is that the first characteristic tone of this vowel corresponds almost completely to the actual data while the second tone given by Rousselot remains beyond the modern pronunciation characteristics. Meanwhile its variant [ỵ] described by this scientist as an open variant (*ü* moyen) almost entirely coincides with the modern [y] F2 characteristics. This observation leads us to check the characteristic tones of the both variants of this vowel suggested by Rousselot with modern listener's perception.

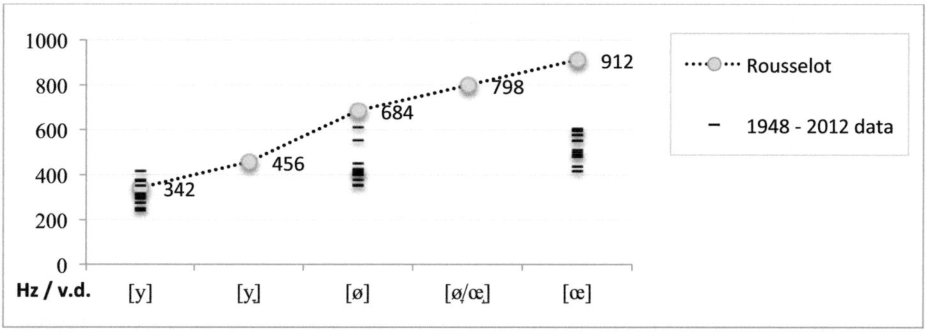

Figure 5. F1 of the French front rounded oral vowels, data from 1948 until 2012, in Hz (isolated hyphen markers) vs. 1st characteristic tone given by Rousselot in v.d. [22] (continuous dotted line)

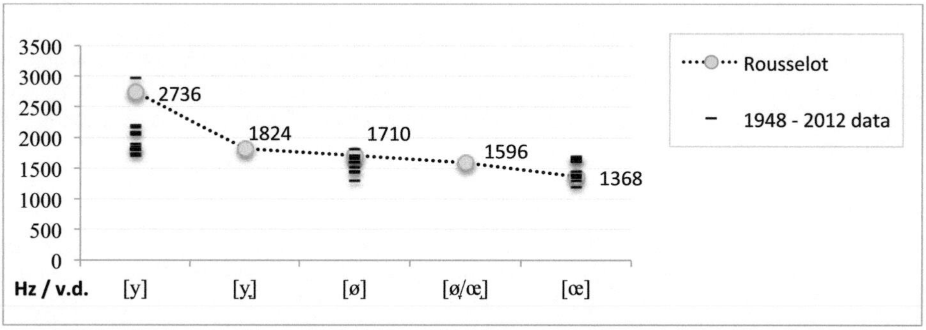

Figure 6. F2 of the French front rounded oral vowels, data from 1948 until 2012, in Hz (isolated hyphen markers) vs. 2nd characteristic tone given by Rousselot in v.d. [22] (continuous dotted line)

4 Auditory perception experiment

4.1 Materials and methods

Two synthesized sounds were obtained through digital signal processing. These sounds corresponded to Rousselot's description of the two characteristic tones of [y] (*ü fermé*) and [y̞] (*ü moyen*). For this purpose the intervals with the duration of one second were extracted from the middle of the corresponding tuning fork recordings. It allowed to avoid additional noise and non-fundamental frequencies. Then these two extracts were juxtaposed and normalized in such a way that the upper tone to be about half of the lower tone amplitude. Obtained compound sounds were presented to the two native French speakers. The subjects are a man from Provence region and a woman from Lorraine region. Both of them are teachers of the FLE (Français Langue Étrangère) with different levels of musical education. These subjects were asked to answer if the sound they heard was similar to any vowel of their language, and if so, to indicate the vowel. Besides these two synthesized sounds, two more series were demonstrated. One of them consisted of four extracts from the recordings of the tuning forks with engraved values of 1228, 342, 1824 and 2736 v.d.. The length of these four stimuli was the same as in the previous series, i.e. one second. The last series comprised three different sounds produced by the sets of the tuning forks from the collection. Firstly, the tuning forks with values of 342 and 2736 v.d. were activated by a wooden hammer in the presence of the subjects. The tuning forks of 456 and 1824 v.d., then those of 798 and 1596 v.d. were presented in the same way. The last stimulus was the sound produced by the smallest tuning fork from the collection (of 3648 v.d.) activated likewise the previous sets. All stimuli were repeated three times. The both subjects listened to the sound material at the same time.

4.2 Results

The interesting fact is that the listeners were able to accomplish the suggested task and tried to associate such non-natural sounds with certain vowels. Nevertheless among ten demonstrated sounds only three were recognized unanimously. Such conformity was observed for the synthesized sound which included transformed recordings of the tuning forks of 456 and 1824 v.d.. Thus, the sound which corresponded to an unstressed "middle" [y̞] in Rousselot's description was perceived as the "close" [y]. One of the subjects explained that he perceived this sound as the [y] in a stressed open syllable. However, such suggestion may be explained as the result of the sound sample length. The crucial fact is that listeners can hardly put in parallel a sound with a length of one second with a short vowel in an unstressed position. At the same time the sound which corresponded to the description of the stressed "close" [y] in the early 20th century was not recognized by any subject. The answers were [i] and [ɛ̃]. The extraction from the recording of the tuning fork of 2736 v.d. defined by Rousselot as "middle" [i̞] was unanimously perceived as [i]. The same answers were observed for the sound of the activated isolated tuning fork of 3648 v.d. which represented the "close" [i]. These results only partially correlate with observations made by Rousselot and may witness of a change of the French vowel system.

5 Conclusion

The results of the current study show that the experimental technique of vowel identification by one or two characteristic tones which uses recorded tuning fork sounds is still valid. This may be achieved not only by a well-trained phonetician, but also by a modern naïve native speaker. Furthermore, the comparison of Rousselot's description with the modern instrumental data leads us to several conclusions. Firstly, F1 and, especially, F2 values of some vowels are approximate to the characteristic tones given by Rousselot. At the same time, the modern formant measurements of [i] described in the early 20th century as the "close i" still crucially differ from the values suggested by J. P. Rousselot. The same relation is observed for the second formant of [y] (the “close ü”). However, compared to the recent data [14, 20], characteristic tone of [i] is apparently very close to its F3 meaning. It allows us to suppose that Rousselot perceived the F3 as the dominant tone of [i]. Such inference also correlates with the data of another recent formant characteristics’ study [13]. Auditory experiment’s results demonstrate that the modern [y] corresponds more to its open variant in Rousselot’s description. As it can be seen from the modern data (mentioned above), the close vowels [u], [i] and [y] became more open during the last century. This fact may be caused by entirely linguistic reasons as well as by anthropological changes, such as the increasing height of the human race in general. Thus, in the accomplished study one century old acoustic devices and methods are applied along with the new instrumental analysis and signal processing procedure. That allows us to suggest that the experimental technique used in the earlier days of acoustic phonetics, instead of being a museum issue, remains useful today. It enables reconstructing some old methodologies and investigating the pronunciation of earlier times. Therefore, it gives an insight into the sound system functioning and evolution.

6 References

[1] BEYER, R. T.: *Sounds of our times: two hundred years of acoustics*, Springer, New York, 1999.

[2] BICKERTON, R. C. AND G. S. BARR: *The origin of the tuning fork, Journal of the Royal Society of Medecine*, vol. 80; pp. 771–773, 1987.

[3] BONDARKO, L. AND L. VERBICKAIA: *Un linguiste de l’âge d’argent toujours actuel, Cahiers de l’ILSL,* N 43, pp. 13 – 20, 2015.

[4] BOTHOREL, A., P. SIMON, F. WIOLAND AND J. P. ZERLIG: *Cinéradiographie des voyelles et consonnes du français, Travaux de l’Institut de phonétique de Strasbourg,* Strasbourg, 1986.

[5] CALLIOPE, J. P. TUBACH (réd.): *La parole et son traitement automatique, Collection techniques et scientifiques des télécommunications,* Masson, Paris, 1989.

[6] CGPM: *Comptes rendus des séances de la 11ème conférence générale des poids et mesures* (1960), p. 87, Gauthier-Villars, Paris, 1961.

[7] CHLADNI, E. F. F.: *Traité d’accoustique,* Courciez, Paris, 1809.

[8] DEBROCK, M. AND G. FORREZ: *Analyse mathématique des voyelles orales du néerlandais et du français: methode et résultats, Revue de phonétique appliquée,* vol. 37, pp. 27 – 73, 1976.

[9] DELATTRE, P.: *An acoustic and articulatory study of vowel reduction in four languages, International Review of Applied Linguistics in Language Teaching,* N7 (1), pp. 295 – 326, 1969.

[10] DELATTRE, P.: *Un triangle acoustique des voyelles orales du français, French Review,* vol. 21 (6), pp. 477 – 484, 1948.

[11] DELATTRE, P.: *Comparing the phonetic features of English, French, German and Spanish,* Chilton and Heidelberg, Julius Groos, New York, 1965.

[12] GENDROT, C. AND M. ADDA-DECKER: *Impact of duration on F1/F2 formant values of oral vowels: an automatic analysis of large broadcast news corpora in French and German, Interspeech*, September, 4 – 8, pp. 2453–2456, Lisbon, 2005.

[13] GENDROT, C., M. ADDA-DECKER AND J. VAISSIÈRE: *Les voyelles /i/ et /y/ du français: focalisation et variations formantiques, XXVIIèmes Journées d’étude de la parole,* pp. 2005–208, Avignon, 2008.

[14] GEORGETON, L., N. PAILLEREAU, S. LANDRON, J. GAO AND T. KAMIYAMA: *Analyse formantique des voyelles orales du français en contexte isolé: à la recherche d’une reference pour les apprenants FLE, Actes de la conference conjointe JEP-TALN-RECITAL,* vol. 1: JEP, pp. 145–152, 2012.

[15] GORDINA, M. V., *Istoriïa foneticheskih ucheniï (ot antichnosti do nashih dneï),* Philological Faculty of the Saint Petersburg University, Saint Petersburg, 2006
[16] GUTH, G.: *Contribution à l'étude de la structure acoustique des voyelles du français, Travaux de l'Institut de phonétique de Strasbourg,* N 1, 1968 – 1969.
[17] HELMHOLTZ, H.: *Théorie physiologique de la musique, fondée sur l'étude des sensations auditives*, Victor Masson et fils, Paris, 1868.
[18] KOENIG, R.: *Quelques expériences d'acoustique,* A. Lahure, Paris, 1882.
[19] MACKECHNIE, CH. A., J. J. GREENBERG, R. C. GERKIN, A. A. MACCALL, B. E. HIRSCH, J. D. DURRANT AND Y. RAZ: *Rinne revisited: steel versus aluminum tuning forks*, *Otolaryngology*, vol. 149 (6); pp. 907–913, 2013.
[20] MAUROVA PAILLEREAU, N.: *Perception et production des voyelles orales du français par des futures enseignantes tchèques du FLE, thèse présentée à l'Université Sorbonne nouvelle*, Paris, 2015.
[21] METTAS, O.: *French oral vowels analysed from recorded spontaneous conversations.* In: Ö. LINDBLOM (ed.): *Frontiers of speech communication research,* pp. 93 – 108, Academic Presse, New York, 1979.
[22] ROUSSELOT, P. AND F. LACLOTTE: *Précis de prononciation française,* H. Welter, Paris, 1902.
[23] ROUSSELOT, P. AND F. LACLOTTE: *Premiers elements de prononciation française,* H. Welter, Paris, Leipzig, 1903.
[24] ROUSSELOT, P.: *Modifications phonétiques du langage étudiées dans le patois d'une famille de Cellfrouin (Charentes)*, H. Welter, Paris, 1891.
[25] ROUSSELOT, P.: *Phonétique expérimentale et surdité, La parole: revue internationale de rhinologie, otologie, laryngologie et phonétique exprérimentale*, pp. 7 – 217, 1903.
[26] ROUSSELOT, P.: *Principes de phonétique expérimentale,* vol. 1, H. Welter, Paris, 1897-1901.
[27] ROUSSELOT, P.: *Principes de phonétique expérimentale,* vol. 2, Nouvelle edition, H. Didier, Paris, 1925.
[28] SCHERBA, L.V.: *Russkiïe glasniïe v kachestvennom i kolichestvennom otnoshenii,* U.N. Erlih, Saint Petersburg, 1912.
[29] STEVENS, J. R. AND T. J. PFANNENSTIEL: *The otologist's tuning fork examination – are you striking correctly? Otolaryngology*, vol. 152 (3); pp. 477 – 479, 2015.
[30] STRAKA, G.: *Album phonétique,* Presses Universitaires Laval, Québec, 1965.
[31] ŠTURM, P.: *The Prague historical collection of tuning forks: A surviving replica of the Koenig tonometre, First International Workshop on the History of Speech Communication Research (HSCR 2015),* September, 4 – 5, pp. 95 – 105, Dresden, 2015.
[32] VIGNAL, M. (DIR.): *Dictionnaire de la musique: la musique des origines à nos jours,* Larousse, Paris, 1994.
[33] VIHANTA, V. V.: *Les voyelles toniques du français et leur realisation et perception par les étudiants finnophones,* Jyväskylä, 1965.

Chiba and Kajiyama measured 3D configurations of the human vocal tract and made physical models based on the measurements

Takayuki Arai

Sophia University, Japan
arai@sophia.ac.jp

Abstract: In 1930's, Chiba and Kajiyama conducted 3D measurements of the human vocal tract for the first time in history. In this paper, we first reviewed how they measured vocal-tract configurations. They further simplified the vocal-tract configurations and made physical straight models based on the simplifications. In addition to introducing our replicas of the straight models based on their simplifications, we also designed bent models based on their 3D measurements.

1 Introduction

Chiba and Kajiyama published "The Vowel, Its Nature and Structure" in 1941-42 [1]. This book is considered as one of the classics in the modern speech science, because this book integrated the mechanisms of vowel production and perception from the viewpoints of physiology, physics and psychology in a single book [2,3]. In this book, they first analyzed the voice source in Part 1. In Part 2, they applied Fourier analysis to obtain vowel spectra and discussed the theory of simple resonators, their equivalent electric networks, and basic aspects of vocal tract configuration. In Part 3, they measured vocal tract configurations by using X-ray photography, palatography, and laryngoscopic observation of the pharynx [4]. Then, they calculated the spectra from the cross-sectional area functions of vowels [2]. They even computed the distribution of volume and particle velocities in each vocal tract. Finally, they dicussed human perception of vowels in Part 4. Around 1950, Kenneth N. Stevens came across *The Vowel* at MIT [5]. When Gunnar Fant visited MIT, he encountered *The Vowel*, as well. Chiba and Kajiyama viewed the mechanisms of vowel production from phonation and articulation [3]. This view merged with the filter theory and lead to the Fant's source-filter theory [6]. It also helped him to process X-ray data of Russian speech sounds [6].

In this paper, we first review how Chiba and Kajiyama conducted 3D measurements of the vocal-tract configurations. Then, our replicas of the straight models based on the their simplifications of the measurements are introduced. Finally, we design bent models based on their 3D measurements.

2 3D measurement of the vocal tract configurations

Chiba and Kajiyama used the most advanced technologies at the time including the X-ray imaging device, combined with palatography and laryngoscopic ovservation of the pharynx, and measured the 3D vocal tract configurations.

2.1 Plane vs. solid palatograms

After pronunciation, a palate with powder shows a pattern of regions where the tongue has touched against the palate. Chiba and Kajiyama called it as "plane palatograms." They also claimed that this kind of palatograms shows heavy variability due to the speaker individuality. Therefore, they made "solid" palatograms, instead.

Figure 1 shows two artificial palates: positive and negative. Figure 2 shows cross-sections of negative artificial palate. They were used to estimate the configuration of the oral cavity.

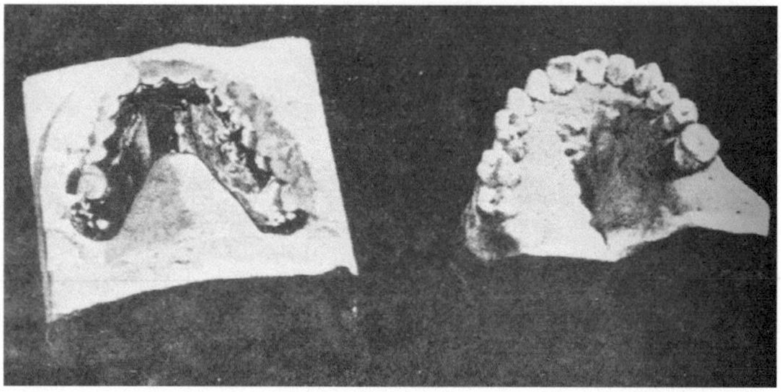

Figure 1. Two artificial palates: positive and negative (from Fig. 62, Chiba and Kajiyama [1]).

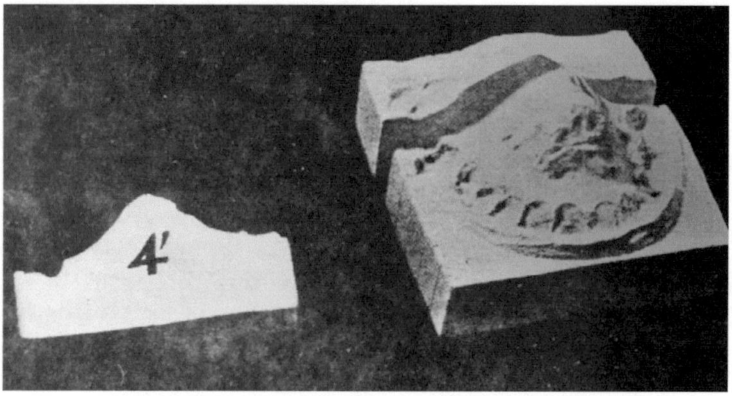

Figure 2. Cross-sections of negative artificial palate (from Fig. 63, Chiba and Kajiyama [1]).

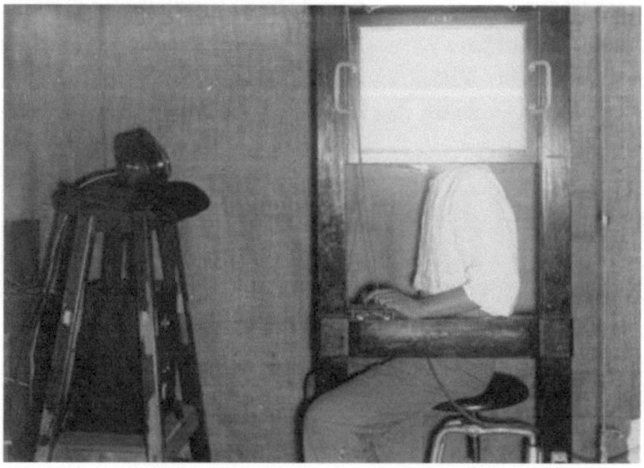

Figure 3. One of the pictures of "Old Phonetics Lab." at the Tokyo School of Foreign Languages (from the archive at the Phonetics Laboratory, Sophia University).

2.2 X-ray imaging

The X-ray imaging device used in *The Vowel* was one of the most state-of-the-art models at that time and made by Shimadu. Figure 3 shows a picture of "Old Phonetics Lab." at the Tokyo School of Foreign Languages, where Chiba and Kajiyama conducted experiments for *The Vowel* from 1934 through 1939.

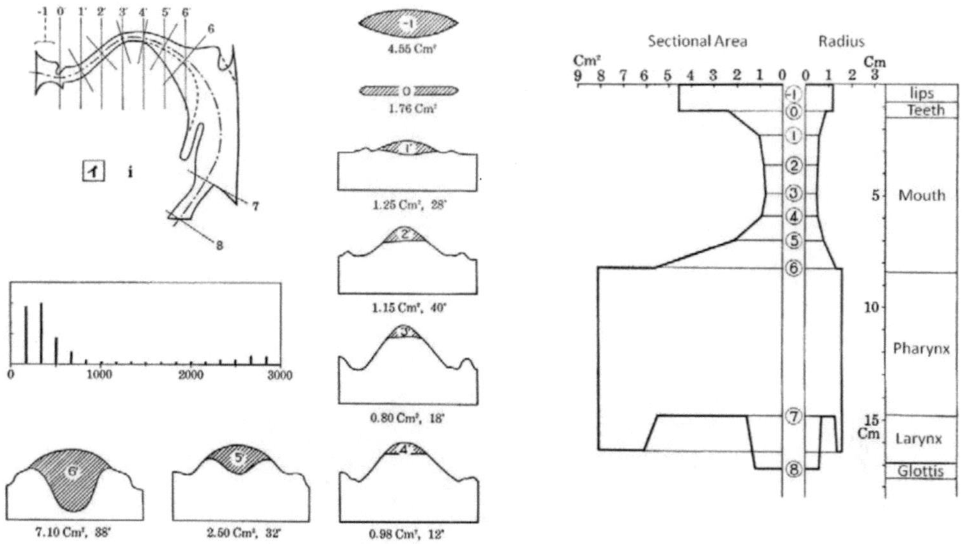

Figure 4. Left: sections of vocal tract of Japanese vowels /i/. Right: simplified dimensions for vowel /i/. (Figs. 68 and 69, Chiba and Kajiyama [1]).

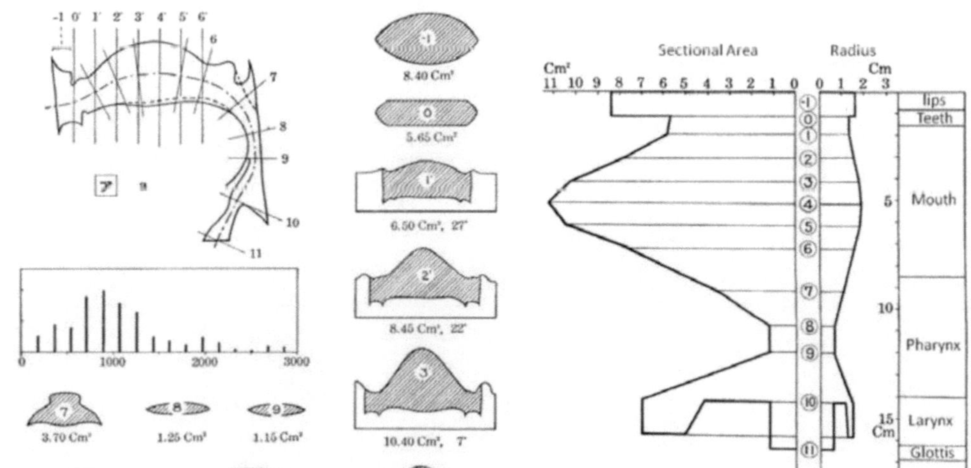

Figure 5. Left: sections of vocal tract of Japanese vowels /a/. Right: simplified dimensions for vowel /a/. (Figs. 68 and 69, Chiba and Kajiyama [1]).

2.3 Sections of vocal tract

Figures 4 and 5 are Figures 68, 69, 72 and 73 in *The Vowel*. The left panels in Figures 4 and 5 show sections of vocal tract of Japanese vowels /i/ and /a/ obtained from the combination of X-ray photography, palatography, and laryngoscopic observation of the pharynx. The right panels in Figures 4 and 5 are the simplified dimensions for these two vowels.

3 Physical models of the human vocal tract

3.1 Replicas of the straight models

In 2001, we celebrated the 60th anniversary of the publication of *The Vowel* and replicated Chiba and Kajiyama's straight models originally described in their book [7]. Starting from page 128, there is a section of "Artificial Vowels" with description of their physical models being able to produce vowels resembling to natural sounds [1]. Figure 6 shows the replicas of the straight models. In Arai [7], we also demonstrated that the physical models of the human vocal tract is very useful and effective for education in speech science and acoustic phonetics. Please see [8,9,10] for further discussions.

Figure 6. Replicas of Chiba and Kajiyama's straight models (from left, /i/, /e/, /a/, /o/ and /u/).

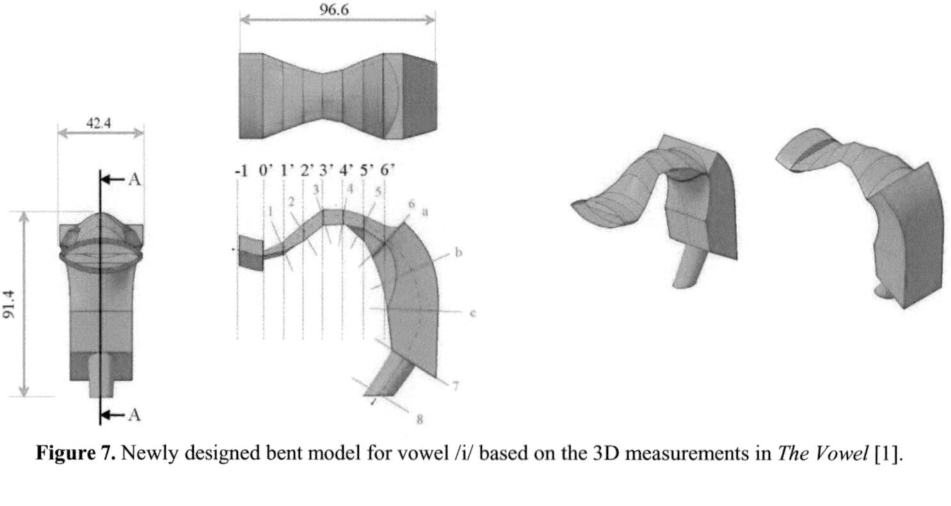

Figure 7. Newly designed bent model for vowel /i/ based on the 3D measurements in *The Vowel* [1].

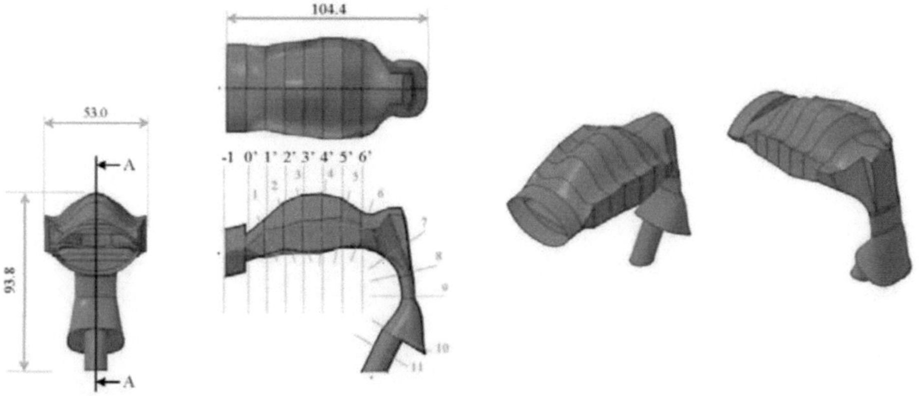

Figure 8. Newly designed bent model for vowel /a/ based on the 3D measurements in *The Vowel* [1].

3.2 Designing bent models based on the 3D measurements

In this paper, we further designed bent models based on the 3D measurements by Chiba and Kajiyama. Figures 7 and 8 show the designs of vowels /i/ and /a/ by combining dimensions in Figures 4 and 5, respectively. Although Chiba and Kajiyama drew outlines of the uvula, epiglottis, and piriform fossa, we omitted them for the designs in these figures.

4 Summary

In this paper, we first reviewed *The Vowel* by Chiba and Kajiyama including how they measured configurations of the human vocal tract. Their simplifications of the measured vocal-tract configurations were also reviewed. Not only our early replicas of the straight models based on their simplifications were introduced, but bent models based on their original 3D measurements were newly designed. These days, computer models are widely available, and we know they are useful in pedagogical settings as well. However, we also showed that producing vowels through physical models is intuitive and still educational for all ages. Newly proposed physical models are more realistic because they are bent and towards simple anatomy. Thus, both straight and bent simple models are useful depending on how we use them for educational purposes, and we still benefit from *The Vowel* by Chiba and Kajiyama, after more than 75 years of its publication.

5 Acknowledgments

I would like to thank the following people for their support: Michael Ashby (UCL); Tsutomu Sugawara, Shigeko Shinohara, Mayako Niikura, Mafuyu Kitahara, and Tomohiko Ooigawa (Sophia Univ.). It was partially supported by JSPS KAKENHI Grant Number 15K00930.

References

[1] Chiba, T., and M. Kajiyama: *The Vowel: Its Nature and Structure*, Tokyo-Kaiseikan, Tokyo, 1941-42.

[2] Maekawa, K., and K. Honda: *On the Vowel, Its Nature and Structure and related works by Chiba and Kajiyama*, *J. Phonetic Soc. Jpn.*, 5(2), pp. 15–30, 2001.

[3] Arai, T.: *History of Chiba and Kajiyama and their influence in modern speech science, From Sound to Sense*, MIT, 2004.
[4] Maekawa, K.: *From articulatory phonetics to the physics of speech: Contribution of Chiba and Kajiyama, Acoust. Sci. Tech.*, 23(4), pp. 185–188, 2002.
[5] Stevens, K. N.: *The Chiba and Kajiyama book as a precursor to the acoustic theory of speech production, J. Phonetic Soc. Jpn.*, 5(2), pp. 6–7, 2001.
[6] Fant, G.: *T. Chiba and M. Kajiyama, pioneers in speech acoustics, J. Phonetic Soc. Jpn.*, 5(2), pp. 4–5, 2001.
[7] Arai, T.: *The replication of Chiba and Kajiyama's mechanical models of the human vocal cavity, J. Phonetic Soc. Jpn.*, 5(2), pp. 31–38, 2001.
[8] Arai, T.: *Education system in acoustics of speech production using physical models of the human vocal tract, Acoust. Sci. Tech.*, 28(3), pp. 190–201, 2007.
[9] Arai, T.: *Education in acoustics and speech science using vocal-tract models, J. Acoust. Soc. Am.*, 131(3), Pt. 2, pp. 2444–2454, 2012.
[10] Arai, T.: *Vocal-tract models and their applications in education for intuitive understanding of speech production, Acoust. Sci. Tech.*, 37(4), pp. 148–156, 2016.

ORIGINS OF SOURCE FILTER THEORY FROM MERSENNE (1636) TO MÜLLER (1839)

Daniel Aalto[1,2]
[1]*Communication Sciences and Disorders*
Faculty of Rehabilitation Medicine, University of Alberta
[2]*Institute for Reconstructive Sciences in Medicine*
Misericordia Community Hospital, Edmonton, Canada
aalto@ualberta.ca

Abstract: Source filter theory is central in the modern description of speech production. The key concepts underpinning the theory are the sustained oscillation of vocal folds and the vocal tract resonances that modulate the source signal. In this short essay the development of these concepts is superficially followed from early 17th to late 19th century. Marin Mersenne was the first to experimentally verify the relationship between the pitch of a sound (of a cord) and its fundamental frequency, published in 1636. By analogy, Mersenne concluded that vocal folds must vibrate with the same frequency as a string with the same pitch. While Mersenne could not explain why several frequencies could be simultaneously present in glottal excitation, Daniel Bernoulli suggested superposition of waves as a solution in 1753, which was further developed by Joseph Fourier. Johannes Müller's report of excised larynx experiments in 1839 can be considered as the first version of source filter theory. Finally, once X-ray imaging during speech production was made possible in 1897, the stage was set for experimental validation of source filter theory.

1 Introduction

The main events that contributed to the creation of source filter theory can be traced back to key experiments and theoretical developments that are documented in books, correspondence, and journal articles. However, limited availability and accessibility of written sources may distort the story that emerges.

In preparing this essay, the author has sought both original sources and earlier descriptions of related historical trajectories. The original sources include Mersenne's Harmonie Universelle [1], Daniel Bernoulli's Hydrodynamica and medical writings [2], Fourier's paper on heat conduction [3], Willis's theory of vowels [4], and Müller's book on physiology (English translation) and his paper on excised larynges [5, 6]. In all historical texts automated search with suitable anatomical (e.g., larynx, vocal folds, etc.) and acoustic keywords (e.g., vibration, resonance, etc.) were used to limit detailed reading to relevant content. In addition to the original historical sources, descriptions of them were used to create a balanced interpretation of the sources in their historical and scientific context. Parallel historical trajectories describing the development of pitch perception models [7], general acoustics [8, 9], speaking machines [10], and vowel production studies [11] were used to identify when and how related concepts emerged to guide the interpretation of the texts regarding speech production.

2 Marin Mersenne and fundamental frequency

Marin Mersenne (1588–1648) is usually credited for determining the relationship between frequency and pitch of a vibrating string [8]. He attended to a school run by Jesuit priests in France, the same school where René Descartes was accepted a few years later [12, p. 16]. Robert Lenoble characterizes Mersenne as the secretary of the scientists of the time. True, Mersenne had a vast correspondence (compiled later by Armand Beaulieu to fourteen thick volumes) with his contemporaries. Hence, many of the ideas presented by Mersenne reflect the collective knowledge of the scientists of the time.

This is particularly true for Harmonie Universelle, a monograph published in 1636 describing in detail the theory of music and practical instructions regarding interpretation of music (e.g. embellishments) and performance technique including instrumental and singing music. Musical theory is summarized by Mersenne under title *Abregé de la Musique speculative* (adjusted following Cohen [13, p. 100]) as

1. Sound is nothing but a percussion (literally: "beating") of the air, taken up by the sense of hearing when it [the ear] is touched by it [the sound]. Loudness is proportional to the amount of air struck; pitch is proportional to the number of percussions per unit time.

2. The relative sweetness of the consonances is determined by how often the percussions that make up their sounds coincide.

3. The relative sweetness of the consonances is calculated as follows. If the percussions of a certain interval unite, for example, every second time (the octave), it is sweeter than if they unite, for instance, every third time (the fifth).

4. Given a string of a certain length, thickness, and material, quadrupling its tension makes its sound rise one octave.

5. The velocity of straight sound is 453 meters per second independent of loudness and the direction of the wind; the echo's velocity is 319 meters per second.

The significance of Mersenne's work is in compiling the existing knowledge about sound and music to one work and in advancing the knowledge by experimentally establishing the connection between frequency and pitch. In the argument, Mersenne describes the Pythagoran law (frequency is inversely proportional to the length of a string) and goes into further detail relating the tension and the mass of the string to the pitch. This law was first described by Beeckman in 1616, communicated to Descartes in 1618 who was in constant correspondence with Mersenne [12, p. 483]. However, sometimes Galileo is attributed as the inventor of the law [8, pp. xii–xiii], potentially because Mersenne was promoting Galileo's ideas.

To experimentally test the laws of the vibrating strings, Mersenne produced a series of strings that were predicted to have a theoretical pitch difference of exactly one octave. As the strings got longer, there was some discrepancy between the observation and the formula [1, 1.III, propos. XIII, p. 187]. As a byproduct, Mersenne noted that the lowest audible frequency was twenty beats per second [1, 1.III, propos. V, p. 170]. At the same page Mersenne noted that with very long strings (seventeen foot) there is no audible sound, but on the other hand the frequency of the oscillations is visible and can be counted by eye. This remarkable experiment defined through the chain of octaves the frequency of the pitch.

The Harmonie Universelle is divided into two parts each consisting of multiple "books" (fr. *livre*). The fundamental frequency of a vibrating string was derived in detail in the third book. The reasoning was strictly deductive with an emphasis on the logical validity of the steps. However, as explained by Cohen, where Galileo and Descartes soughted certainty fitting with the deductive writing style of the time, Mersenne aimed at precision. When experimental evidence was at odds with universal laws, Mersenne acknowledged the discrepancy. As an example, Mersenne studied the difference between theoretical predictions in his vibrating string formulas and the frequencies of oscillating cords and found a general second order correction factor accounting for the deviations [13, p. 101].

Mersenne and his contemporaries Descartes and Galileo shared a mechanistic view of physiology: the body was operated by a spirit living in the brain. While Mersenne's exploration of senses, in particular vision and the function of the eye, was accurate and neutral with respect to the metaphysical considerations of the mind, he was not very well read in the biological literature of the time [12, pp. 499–502]. Instead of relating his work to that literature, Mersenne chose to describe how the human machine was operated to produce sound from a mechanistic point of view. Mersenne reserved almost one hundred pages to describe the human voice. He opened the book by briefly explaining the structural parts and their roles (adapted from [1, Traitez de la voix et des chants, I, p. 1]):

> The parts that produce voice are called the lungs to push air, windpipe to conduct the air, larynx with an opening resembling a reed of a flute, palate whose concavity makes air or sound to resonate, gargareon (uvula), tongue which forms speech (*parole*) by its movement, front teeth serving the voice production by letting tongue touch them, air without which all the other parts would be nothing, and the mouth of which the lips form most of the letters that are called consonants, in particular the ones that the Hebrews call *labials*.

Mersenne used three dimensions to describe the voice: weak-strong (*foible & forte*), clear-hoarse (*claire & rauque*), and flat-sharp, i.e. low-high (*grave & aigue*) [1, Traitez de la voix et des chants, I, prop. IV, p. 6]. Mersenne explained that

> the strong [voice] resulted from violent movement of the thoracic muscles, the clear [voice] from well regulated humidity in cartilages, membranes, and the laryngeal muscles, and the hoarse from too great humidity or dryness of the same parts.

In explaining the vocal fold relationship to the fundamental frequency, Mersenne used an analogue to the flute and pipe organ. The long descriptions of intralaryngeal muscles and their role in regulating the phonation reveal that Mersenne was able to correctly deduce the impact of various muscles on phonation. These reasonings were based by intuitive application of knowledge gained from musical instruments.

Mersenne applied the voice production theory that he had developed to various questions. For instance, in the proposition XXII he asked whether an individual can produce two voices simultaneously, in proposition XXIX he explained how to build a parabola that collects sounds from different locations in a room to one focal point, in proposition XLVIII he discussed the amount of possible and producible sound combinations given the vowels and consonants in a language, and in the proposition LI he described how to help deaf children to learn to speak.

All the topics chosen for discussion were thoroughly treated with an easy-to-follow logic. A long explanation was devoted to articulatory description of different "letters" by place of articulation [1, Traitez de la voix et des chants, I, proposition XLIII, p. 56–59]. Mersenne explained that five vowels, *a, e, o, i, u* were sufficient to derive a vowel in any language by interpolating between *a* and the other four. For these five vowels he described the characteristic positions of the tongue and the lips. Mersenne emphasized that the roles of larynx and supraglottal articulators were distinct:

> Or il faut premierement remarquer que les voyelles ne se forment pas par la seule ouuerture du larynx, & de la glotte, qui n'a nulle autre vertu que de former les sons graues & aigus, forts & foibles, clairs, & rauques, &c. car les sons ne seroient nulle voyelle si l'on n'auoit point de langue, dont le plus simple abbaissement qui se fait

au bout forme la premier voyelle A, lors qu'elle s'estend, & qu'elle soustient le son; l'O se fait quasi par la mesme situation de la langue, car elle se retire & s'enfle fort peu vers le milieu du palais [1].

As much as Mersenne provided insight to the human voice production, he could not explain why multiple frequencies could be heard simulatenously in the human voice and in vibrating strings. However, Mersenne's description of speech production was articulatorily accurate with conceptual separation of vocal source and vocal tract. In particular, Mersenne was the first to quantify phonation in terms of the frequency of glottal pulses.

3 Daniel Bernoulli and Joseph Fourier

Daniel Bernoulli (1700–1782) is best known for his work in hydrodynamics that he published in 1738. However, before devoting his time to physics, he studied medicine graduating in 1720, and wrote a doctoral dissertation about respiration in Basel in 1721 [2, V. Zimmermann in Part 1, p. 6]. After working as a physician in Italy for two years [14], he moved to St Petersburg to serve in the Academy of Sciences where he worked with Leonhard Euler and began writing Hydrodynamica [15, G.K. Mikhailov in Chapter 9]. In 1733, he returned to Basel as a professor in anatomy and botany. Although Bernoulli's passion was clearly in mathematics and physics, his contribution to medicine was substantial, including a treatise on muscular mechanics (1726), and on mechanical work done by the heart (1737, 1748) [2]. Bernoulli did not directly address blood circulation or airflow in the respiratory system in *Hydrodynamica* although the principles presented in the book directly apply to these physiological situations and left a permanent trace into the history of medicine [14].

The relevance of Bernoulli's work to source filter theory is twofold. First, the Bernoulli principle was presented in *Hydrodynamica* and later applied to glottal flow and sustained vocal folds vibration [16]. Second, Bernoulli introduced the concept of superposition of waves (as explained by Robert Lindsay in [8, p. xv]) in 1755 that was crucial in shaping the theory of Fourier.

Joseph Fourier (1768–1830) presented his solution of the heat equation based on spectral decomposition, i.e. as an infinite sum of trigonometric functions, to the Institut de France in 1807. It was not received well by Laplace and Lagrange and the paper was published much later [17]. However, it soon became a well respected manuscript in mathematics [15, Chapter 26]. The mathematical challenges in handling infinite series of trigonometric functions inspired a considerable amount of mathematical work. Earlier, the analysis of the vibrating string by d'Alembert had already sparked a controversy about the definition of a function in 1747 and got intertwined with the problems of convergence in early 19th century. The interrelated mathematical concepts and arguments are described in detail by Gonzalez-Velasco [17].

As Fulop points out, the value of Fourier's work was in generalizing the earlier superposition concepts of Euler and Bernoulli and in creating an integral transform that could handle aperiodic signals as well [18]. However, it was not until 1966 before the convergence problems in the Fourier's theory were finally solved by Lennart Carleson [19].

To conclude, both Daniel Bernoulli and Joseph Fourier pushed their respective fields forward and created mathematical tools and concepts that became instrumental to speech production research. However, there appears to be no direct evidence to demonstrate that they would

[1] But first a remark has to be made that vowels are not formed just by opening larynx, and the glottis, which have no other quality than to form low and high, strong and weak, clear and rough, etc. sounds, since the sounds would be no vowels at all if one has no tongue, which forms the first vowel A if simply lowered to the bottom, as it extends and supports the sound; the O is produced at the almost same tongue position, since it retracts and expands only little towards the middle of the palate.

have applied their knowledge to the human voice.

4 Johannes Müller and excised larynges

Johannes Müller (1801–1858) was a prominent anatomist and physiologist advocating microscopic research and physiological experimentation. His comprehensive book on human physiology and his experimental paper on excised larynges may be considered the first account of source filter theory [5, 6, 11]. Similar to Mersenne, Müller synthesized knowledge of his field together with advancing it with new experimental evidence.

Müller summarized the speech production acoustics in the following [6, p. 695]:

> The circumstance of the vocal tube in front of the vocal cords being double, consisting of the oral and nasal canals, seems to have no other effect on the height of the notes than a simple tube; but it causes their character to be altered by the resonance. I attached to the short anterior tube of an artificial larynx with caoutchouc tongues a bifurcated tube; the result was no raising of the notes, but they were rendered more sonorous.

In addition to the artificial larynges, Müller used extensively excised human and animal (at least bovine, ovine, and simian) larynges coupled with acoustic tubes. Hence, Müller was able to experimentally verify that the source signal and the vocal tract resonances were, to a large extent, independent of each other. However, Müller mentioned that elongation of the tube that was coupled with the excised larynx lowered the pitch by a semitone, or very rarely, an entire tone [5]. Underlying these reasonings is the observation from musical instruments, in particular reed instruments, that a resonance (usually the lowest) of the instrument forces the frequency of the reed to lock to the resonant frequency. It appears that Müller felt it necessary to explain why such a locking does not take place in the larynx.

At the surface, the earlier quotes from Mersenne and Müller show little difference in their description of the voice production. However, Müller could provide the frequencies of the vocal tract resonances that he observed in his experiments, whereas Mersenne could only describe the frequency of the vocal source oscillations. While Müller was not the first one to determine the frequencies of the vocal tract resonances, he was apparently the first to experimentally study the interaction between vocal fold and vocal tract oscillations. However, Müller never delved into the signal processing of the speech sounds nor mentioned Fourier's work although he extensively cited earlier works in medicine and speech research including Willis's study of vowels [4]. In contrast, Hermann Helmholtz, who was listening to Müller's lectures on anatomy and physiology in Berlin and whom Müller mentored to a successful career in science, managed to bring together the theory of resonance and vowel production [20].

When John Strutt, better known as Lord Rayleigh, published a textbook about acoustics in 1877, Helmholtz asked for him to include speech acoustics as a third volume [21]. Rayleigh followed Helmholtz's advice and expanded the second edition to include a chapter about speech, published in 1894. However, it is clear that a consensus about vowel production mechanisms had not yet been formed.

In 1890's two remarkable developments can be pinpointed that fundamentally impacted the 20th century phonetics. First, anatomical imaging data during vowel production was presented by Max Scheier in the meeting of otolaryngologists less than a year after the invention of the X-ray imaging technology [22, 23]. The new technology later provided crucial data for refining and validating the models of vocal tract acoustics [24]. Second, sound recordings and Fourier analysis of these waveforms became gradually more common establishing the source filter framework through a new concept, the formant [18, pp. 52–56], [25].

5 Conclusions

Source filter theory developed gradually from qualitative, anatomical descriptions of speech production. In the early 17th century Mersenne deduced the fundamental frequency of phonation by analogy, hence drafting the first quantitative account of vowel production. Bernoulli proposed that multiple frequencies may be present in the vibration of a body which Fourier confirmed in the early 19th century theoretically. Müller's work on artificial and excised larynges in 1839 articulated the essence of the source filter theory by observing that resonances of the vocal tract and the vibrating frequency of the vocal folds are largely unrelated. It is noteworthy that the key concepts of vocal source oscillations and spectral filtering were established before sound was ever recorded.

6 Acknowledgments

The author is grateful for Louis Clerc, Gabriela Constantinescu, Fred Cummins, and anonymous reviewers for feedback that improved the manuscript.

References

[1] MERSENNE, M.: *Harmonie Universelle.* Sebastien Cramoisy, Paris (digitally accessible at imslp.org), 1636.

[2] SPEISER, D.: *Die Werke von Daniel Bernoulli.* Birkhäuser, Basel, 1996.

[3] FOURIER, J.: *Théorie analytique de la chaleur.* Firmin Didot, Paris, 1822.

[4] WILLIS, R.: *On the vowel sounds, and on reed organ-pipes. Transactions of the Cambridge pholosophical society*, pp. 231–276, 1830.

[5] MÜLLER, J.: *Über die Compensation der physischen Kräfte am menschlichen Stimmorgan.* A. Hirschwald, Berlin, 1839.

[6] MÜLLER, J.: *Elements of physiology.* Translated from German by W. M. Baly, Lea and Blanchard, Philadelphia, 1843.

[7] DE CHEVEIGNÉ, A.: *Pitch perception models.* In *Plack, C. and Oxenham A. (eds), Pitch*, pp. 169–233. Springer, 2005.

[8] STRUTT, J. W.: *The theory of sound, 2nd ed. revised and enlarged 1894 with a historical introduction by R. B. Lindsay.* Dover Publications, 1929.

[9] ROSSING, T. D.: *Springer Handbook of Acoustics.* Springer, New York, 2007.

[10] FAGYAL, Z.: *Phonetics and speaking machines: on the mechanical simulation of human speech in the 17th century. Historiographia Linguistica*, 28, pp. 289–330, 2001.

[11] HONDA, K.: *Evolution of vowel production studies and observation techniques. Acoustical Science and Technology*, 23(4), pp. 189–194, 2002.

[12] LENOBLE, R.: *Mersenne ou la naissance du mécanisme.* Paris, J. Vrin, 1943.

[13] COHEN, H.: *Quantifying music, the science of music at the first stage of the scientific revolution, 1580–1650.* D. Reidel Publishing Company, Dordrecht, 1984.

[14] FYE, W.: *Profiles in cardiology – Johann and Daniel Bernoulli. Clinical cardiology*, 24, pp. 634–645, 2001.

[15] GRATTAN-GUINNESS, I.: *Landmark writings in Western mathematics, 1640–1940*. Elsevier, 2005.

[16] COOPER, D.: *Voice: a historical perspective; Woldemar Tonndorf and the Bernoulli effect in voice production. Journal of Voice*, 3(1), pp. 1–6, 1989.

[17] GONZELZ-VELASCO, E.: *Connections in mathematical analysis: the case of Fourier series. American Mathematical Monthly*, 99, pp. 427–441, 1992.

[18] FULOP, S. A.: *Speech spectrum analysis*. Springer, 2011.

[19] CARLESON, L.: *On the convergence and growth of parital sums of Fourier series. Acta mathematica*, 116(1), pp. 135–157, 1966.

[20] FINGER, S. and N. J. WADE: *The neuroscience of Helmholtz and the theories of Johannes Müller: Nerve cell structure, vitalism, and the nerve impulse. Journal of the history of the neurosciences*, 11, pp. 136–155, 2002.

[21] HELMHOLTZ, H.: *Book review: The theory of sound. Nature*, 19, pp. 117–118, 1878.

[22] SCHEIER, M.: *Anwendung der Röntgenstrahlen für die Physiologie der Stimme und Sprache. Deutsche Medicinische Wochenschrift*, 1897.

[23] DOMMANN, M.: *Durchsicht, Einsicht, Vorsicht – eine Geschichte der Röntgenstrahlen 1896–1963*. Chronos-Verlag, Zurich, 2003.

[24] FANT, G.: *Acoustic theory of speech production*. Mouton, The Hague, 1960.

[25] TITZE, I. R., R. J. BAKEN, K. W. BOZEMAN, S. GRANQVIST, H. HENRICH, C. T. HERBST, D. M. HOWARD, E. J. HUNTER, D. KAELIN, R. D. KENT, and J. KREIMAN: *Toward a consensus on symbolic notation of harmonics, resonances, and formants in vocalization. The Journal of the Acoustical Society of America*, 137(5), pp. 3005–3007, 2015.

FROM *VISIBLE SPEECH* TO VOICEPRINTS – BLESSING AND CURSE OF SOUND SPECTROGRAPHY

Angelika Braun

University of Trier, Germany
brauna@uni-trier.de

Abstract: Sound spectrography is probably the single most widely used tool in acoustic phonetics today. It was first called *Visible Speech,* thus linking it to Alexander Melville Bell's 1867 publication. At that time, of course, the term only referred to auditory analysis and the iconic documentation thereof. During World War II, sound spectrography as we know it today was developed in the US as part of a war project and was therefore not published until well after the war. A similar device was built in the Soviet Union in the post-war period. Although claims were made on both sides that the device was intended for the benefit of the congenitally deaf, it is quite clear that its primary purpose was in speaker identification. This contribution focuses on the development of the sound spectrograph and outlines its role in (forensic) speaker identification.

1 Introduction – Visualizing speech

1.1 The early days

One of the fundamental problems with human speech and its analysis is that it is volatile. Until the late 19th century, there were no technical means of conserving spoken language. The Edison phonograph dates back to 1877, and the gramophone was not developed until ten years later by Emil Berliner. The next step in the conservation of spoken utterances was once again undertaken by Berliner and consisted in the development of shellac disks in 1896. It was not until the 1930s that magnetic tape was used to record longer stretches of sound than would fit on a long play disk. Reel-to-reel tape recorders were largely replaced by tape cassettes in the 1960s, and the era of digital recordings did not start until the 1980s (cf. [33] for an excellent summary).

Attempts at visualizing speech in terms of acoustic dimensions started even later than the development of devices to record it. In the early days of experimental phonetics, various aspects of speech were made visible by way of kymograms. The kymograph could be used to record just about any kind of event over time, be it respiratory movements or volumes, phonation, or certain aspects of articulation as, e.g., nasality. The device consisted of a rotating drum which was covered by paper that had been smoked with petroleum fumes, and a stylus to record various kinds of signals. After the recording process, which could extend to a few seconds at best (depending on the diameter of the drum and the speed at which it rotated), the trace left on the blackened paper had to be fixated by a substance chemically similar to hair spray. The next step in visualization was the cathode ray oscillograph which could be used to depict the time signal in almost real-time.

1.2 The Sound Spectrograph

The single most important device for the visualization of speech and its quantitative analysis, however, was the sound spectrograph (cf., e.g., [23]). Baken and Daniloff [5] call it "a genuine landmark in the phonetic sciences, a birth announcement of a new era" (p. 1). The device consists of a rotating drum which is covered by electrosensitive paper (reminiscent of kymography). In its analog form it uses electronic filtering of the speech signal in order to display the energy which is present in various frequency components over time by means of a moving filter and a stylus etching a pattern into the paper according to frequency and intensity. (For a detailed description cf. [4], pp. 329-345.) The spectrogram will thus depict time (abscissa), frequency (ordinate), and intensity (blackening or – today – color) in a pseudo-3D plot.

The digital age has added a lot of flexibility to spectrographic analysis – the sampling rate, quantization, windowing and the color scheme, to name only a few key parameters, can be adjusted by mouse click. Above all, the speed of the analysis has tremendously increased from taking 2½ minutes for a 2.4 second recording ([19], p.75) to a fraction of a second for long stretches of recorded speech. However, the three dimensions depicted in a spectrogram (time, frequency, and intensity) are still and will remain indispensable for acoustic phonetic analysis. Baken and Daniloff's ([5], p. x) assessment from the early days of the digital age still holds today: "During recent years, speech sound spectrography has become easier, cheaper, and potentially more useful than ever."

2 *Visible speech* and the teaching of the deaf

Being able to record and – in particular – visualize speech was of prime importance for teaching congenitally deaf individuals to speak before the age of cochlear implants. There is a fairly long tradition of efforts in this area in various countries, e.g., Spain (Pedro Ponce de Leon 1516-1584), The Netherlands [2], and England [12; 41]. Somewhat later, Alexander Melville Bell [6] devised a "phonetic" alphabet which was also known as the physiological alphabet. He called it *Visible Speech*. It symbolizes somewhat iconically the positions of the vocal organs during the production of the respective sounds [1]. It was meant to serve as a tool which would allow deaf patients to learn to articulate properly

The following illustration is a projection of Bell's symbols onto the current IPA consonant chart:

251658240

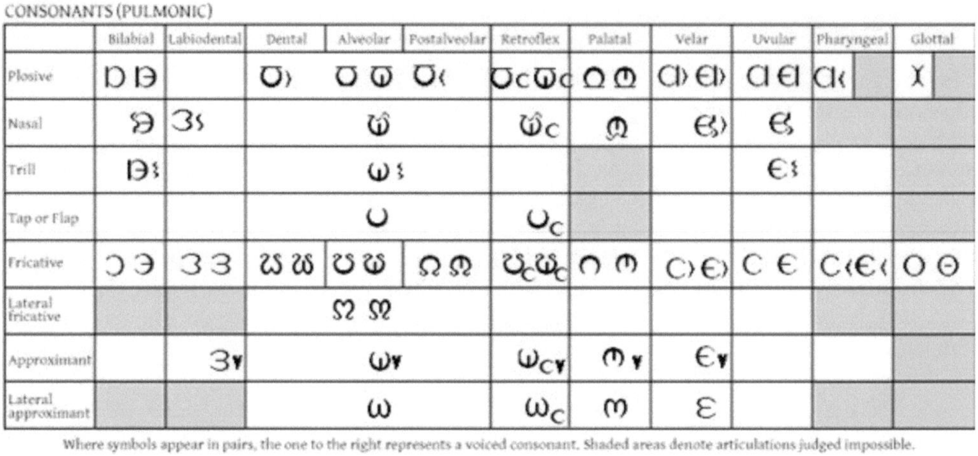

Table 1: IPA consonant chart with *Visible Speech* symbols (www.omniglot.com/writing/visiblespeech.htm)

3 *Visible Speech* revived

3.1 Official reports and publications

The publicly accessible sources on the development of the sound spectrograph are all post-World War II. Those sources [28, 29, 30] demonstrate that even before World War II researchers at Bell Telephone Laboratories in New York, N.Y. (henceforth: Bell Labs) had begun "to replace [...] an extensive array of fixed filters with one adjustably tuned unit" for the purpose of the acoustic analysis of speech ([28], p.1). According to Potter ([29], p.1), "A great deal of patient development work was necessary before the pictures were good enough to show the detail they are able to show today." To be precise, two devices were developed: A "cathode-ray translator [producing] instantaneous but transitory patterns on a phosphorescent screen in a rotating cathode-ray tube" ([19], p. 75; [8], [31]), and the spectrograph producing the kind of pseudo-3D images which are in principle still in use today. The former was not available until "late in 1944" ([30], p.5), whereas "a spectrograph development was started early in 1941" (ibid, p.4). This can be taken as an indication of the relative importance which was attached to those two devices, the spectrograph clearly taking priority.

The latter view is confirmed by Potter et al. ([30], pp.4-5), according to whom the purpose of creating those devices was twofold. "American participation in the war emphasized the military applications of, and needs for, a visual translation of sound, and during the war period major interest was centered upon these military requirements. It was not until military needs had been met that opportunity was offered for a resumption of the development of visible speech toward the goal of visual hearing" ([30], p.5).

Still, the monograph [30] is for the most part devoted to spectrogram reading and thus to the guise of clinical use. All other post-war publications likewise focus on clinical aspects, i.e., they emphasize that the development of the translator in particular occurred with deaf patients in mind. Ostensibly, a prime goal of their war time research was to enable congenitally deaf individuals to use the telephone. In fact, they describe at length how a group of those patients learned to "read" spectrograms ([30], chapters 4, 13). This, however, does not in the least explain the development of the spectrograph. The latter was said to be motivated by "other interests in sound portrayal that are important to those working with sound in all its variations" ([29], p.2). Nowhere in these articles, let alone in the Potter et al. [30] monograph is there any clear indication of a specific use for speaker identification purposes. Instead, there is ample reference to the fact that spectrograms produced by different speakers look alike (e.g., [28], p.465). However, he goes on to remark that "[t]he pattern shapes [...] vary with individual characteristics in much the same way that handwriting varies among individuals" (ibid.). This vague analogy to handwriting, which is much more adequate than that to fingerprints, remains the closest hint at voice comparison efforts in the post-war publications. Kopp and Green ([19] p.87) write: “It is axiomatic that no two individuals have voices that are exactly alike in pitch or vocal quality, but visible speech, in the form considered in this paper, does not emphasize these variables.” Thus, while individuality of speech patterns is assumed, the speaker specificity of sound spectrograms is expressly played down.

3.2 The mysterious report

Contrary to the impression created by, e.g., Kopp and Green [19], it is quite clear that the sound spectrograph was not primarily developed for research purposes. Instead, as early as 1941, a project on speaker identification was initiated by the American Military Forces at that same laboratory. C.H.G. Gray supervised the project until the summer of 1945. According to Potter et al. [30] he was succeeded by J.C. Steinberg, whose work [37] had served as a basis for the development of the spectrograph ([25], p.85).

Potter ([28], p.463) points to the relevance of the project for the war, but does not become specific: "The work here described was begun before the war. Because of related war interests it was given official rating as a war project, [...]". Thus, the project was classified during WW II for obvious reasons, assuming that the rendition given by Tosi ([40], p.67) is correct. At any rate, the early 1940s can be identified as the time when the research unit at Bell Labs working under C.H. Gray succeeded in developing the sound spectrograph.

There are no publications whatsoever currently available from those early days, but reference is made by Tosi [39] and [40] to an internal Bell Labs report from 1944 which apparently summarizes the war-time usage of the spectrograph [10]. Tosi must have had this report at his disposal since he quotes from it extensively ([39], p.415; [40], pp.67f.). Other researchers also mention this source, but it is quite clear that they did not have a chance to look at the original document since the name of the first author is repeatedly and systematically misspelt as Gr**e**y as opposed to Gr**a**y [9, 24]. Hollien [13], p.352) lists a "report *to* Bell Labs" [emphasis mine, AB] by Gray and Kopp [10] among his references, but does not refer to its content in the respective chapter of his book.

In view of the crucial information which, according to Tosi [39; 40], is contained in the alleged report by Gray and Kopp from 1944 [10], the present author has made extensive efforts to acquire a copy of it. Nokia Bell Labs felt unable to either supply a copy or even confirm its existence[1]. Neither the Library of Congress Catalog nor the National Archives and Records Administration (NARA) nor the Naval Research Lab (NRL) nor the NSA Archives Office

[1] Rebecca S. Nadolny of Nokia Bell Labs by email on 01-11-2017.

yielded any result. Thus, the present contribution has to rely on Tosi [39; 40] as a secondary source.

Tosi quickly dismisses the guise of the spectrograph as a device for the congenitally deaf and leaves no doubt as to its military use: "The machine was developed with the primary purpose of helping the military during the war" ([40], p.64). He continues to report that "[h]owever, in 1944, Gray and Kopp found that spectrograms could be applied to the identification of speakers [...]" (ibid, p.67). He attributes the coinage of the term "voiceprinting" to those authors (ibid, p.67) and quotes from their report as follows:

"Much more simple and quantitative than the aural scheme is a technique based upon the Sound Spectrograph, an instrument which makes permanent patterns of speech that can be examined visually in the way fingerprints or handwriting can be examined and can be filed as reference samples." ([10], p.1; after [40], p.67)

According to Tosi ([39], p.415; [40], pp.67f.), the report was concluded as follows:

"Voice print identification seems to offer the[2] possibility of a useful radio intercept feature and one that could be put into use without extensive training or elaborate equipment. As a study of combat conditions in the European and Pacific theaters indicates a need for such identification, it is suggested that a trial voice identification group be established to carry on the work under actual or simulated field conditions to test the conclusions of this laboratory work."

Tosi ([39], p.415) adds that "[t]o the best knowledge of this writer, such a test was not completed because of the end of the war and the problems of recordings."

From these quotations it emerges that the spectrograph was developed primarily with speaker identification in mind. It would seem that the intention was to use it to identify the voices of German radio operators on various vessels in order to be able to track the movements of the enemy's fleet. Based on goniometry and the matching of radio operators with a specific vessel, the movements of the respective vessels could be determined (cf. [40], p.67).

Indirect proof of this use of spectrograms is contained in an internal report [3] which was provided to the present author by Rebecca S. Nadolny, archivist at Bell Labs. This report summarizes the activities related to sound spectrography in the 1940s as follows: "During World War II, acoustics scientists C. H. G. Gray and G. A. Kopp suggested that enemy radio voices might be identified by spectrogram in order to detect the movement of units from place to place" ([3], 214). This entirely confirms the information contained in Tosi [39; 40].

This must have given the American military forces a significant strategic advantage over the enemy and probably formed an incentive for post-war usage as a tool in forensic speaker identification (see below), even though the matter was not publicly followed up in the early post-war years.

Even though this military focus on the development of a device which could display speech in a quasi-three-dimensional way was clearly prevalent during WW II, it was only mentioned in passing in one the – numerous – post war publications on sound spectrography

[2] The definite article is missing in Tosi [39]. Other than that, the wording is identical.

by various researchers from Bell Labs ([28], p.465). An impressive number of publications by different authors ensued in 1946, basically occupying one whole issue of The Journal of the Acoustical Society of America with a preface written by Ralph Potter [29]. They cover various aspects of spectrographic analysis, including technical detail [21; 31; 8] and – once again – the issue of spectrogram reading [38; 19] but there is no mention of using this technique for speaker identification purposes.

Lonnie Smrkovski, one of the prime advocates of voiceprint identification, hints at the voiceprint application in the 1940s, but does not become specific: "World War II provided a catalyst for research in speaker recognition, and Bell Laboratories conducted experiments in an attempt to develop voiceprints as a tool which could be used in the war effort. The war ended before such a method could be developed, and with its termination there did not appear any need for a means of identifying speakers' voices" ([34] pp.5-6).

Meuwly ([25], p.86) reports that precisely this application of sound spectrography was "classified and financed by the army" in the post-war period. Further evidence for the fact that the "voiceprint" technique was indeed commonplace within US Federal agencies shortly after WW II comes from the FBI itself: Koenig ([20], p.2089) remarks that "FBI examiners have used the spectrographic technique since the 1950s [...]." This, of course, leads to the conclusion that the interest in using sound spectrograms as "voiceprints" never ceased to exist, but was kept secret.

4 *Visible Speech* behind the Iron Curtain

It is interesting to note that similar efforts at constructing a device which would allow for comparing visual renditions of verbal utterances were made in Russia at about the same time as in the US. However, the evidence of the construction and use of a sound spectrograph in Russia is of a completely different nature. In his novel *First Circle,* Aleksander Solzhenitsyn describes an episode dating back to December of 1949. The novel is set in a prison camp for experts in various fields, whose assistance was considered useful by the Stalin regime. Therefore, the scientists were held captive but did not face an immediate threat of death.

One of the tasks given to the scientists in 1949 was to develop a device for graphically depicting speech utterances, which could, in turn, be decoded by trained experts or used as an aid for congenitally deaf patients. The description of what they came up with under the guidance of a character called "Rubin" reads like a blueprint of the Bell Labs spectrograph: This starts with its name: *Widimaja retschj* 'Visible Speech'. Even the guise about it being an aid for the deaf is copied. In Chapter 31 of the German edition, the sample utterance which is to be "read" from a spectrogram by the prisoner called Rubin is "*Swukowidy rasreschajut gluchim goworitj po telefonu*" 'Sound diagrams allow deaf persons to speak over the telephone'. This is reminiscent of the description of that same device allowing a congenitally deaf engineer who was trained to read spectrograms in the US to reconstruct the wording: "The translator has [...] provided a means for this congenitally deaf engineer to make and receive telephone calls" ([30], p.25).

It also emerges from Solzhenitsyn's rendition that spectrographic analysis in that particular case was to be used for forensic phonetic purposes. It was called – voiceprint! In chapter 33 Solzhenitsyn writes: "This was really something quite new – catching a criminal using his voiceprint. So far there had only been fingerprints, a science which had taken centuries to develop. Now there was to be a new technique of 'voiceprinting', and it had to be developed in a matter of days." ([36], p.255; [35], p.233; my translation into English, A.B.) Depending on which edition one chooses to look at[3], an anonymous phone call is described to have been made either to the US embassy or a medical doctor, in each case leaking confidential information. The spectrographic analysis served to narrow down the number of suspects from N=5 to N=2 in a closed-set situation, i.e. only a limited number of speakers could have possibly made the phone call in question.

Since this application was hinted at in an unclassified publication by Potter ([28], p.465), it can be speculated how the Russians may have gained access to the technical information which led to the development of the device. At any rate, it does not seem conceivable that Lev Kopelev, who is the scientist represented by the character "Rubin" in the novel, could have built a spectrograph from scratch, let alone within the time span in question. The time at which the novel is set suggests that the Russians were trailing the American scientists in developing a sound spectrograph by about four years if one considers the publicly accessible papers starting with Potter [28] and by eight years if the completion of the device for military purposes is taken into account. This is what gave rise to the above-mentioned speculations on the source of Russian knowledge about the device. It would seem, however, that none of those speculating have ever taken a close look at Solzhenitsyn's original text. He literally says: "Rubin himself had already forgotten that this device had been bootlegged from an American journal." ([36], p.244)[4]. This detail is lacking in the German edition of 1968. It may not be mentioned in the English translation either. A reason for this may be that most translations (the German one for certain) are based on the 1968 edition of the novel, whereas the remark in question is taken from the 1978 edition, which is known to be more comprehensive than the earlier ones. This constitutes indirect proof for the fact that from the start the main purpose of the sound spectrograph was to compare speakers' voices. It finally leaves no doubt as to who first developed the device – these were quite clearly the scientists at Bell Labs, their Russian colleagues lagging behind by close to a decade. Eriksson (n. dat., p. 4) correctly points out that the term "phonoscopy" is still in use in the Eastern European Countries. This is confirmed for Russia by Feruza Bayramova, a Russian speaker identification expert (p.c. April 2017).

5 From *Visible Speech* to "voiceprints"

Up to now, the term "voiceprint" has been closely associated with the name of Lawrence Kersta ([32], p.107; [22], p.58; [13], p.212). And, yet, it may be much older than that, dating back to Gray and Kopp [10], if one chooses to believe Tosi ([39], p.415). Plausibility is added to his version by the fact that it was adopted by Solzhenitsyn before Kersta ever published it. – Still, Lawrence Kersta played a key role in establishing "voiceprints" as courtroom evidence, which merits looking at in more detail.

5.1 The role of Lawrence Kersta

In their preface to the first edition of *Visible Speech*, Potter, Kopp, and Green [30] pay tribute to all members of the group of scientists who took part in the development of the sound spectrograph (p. viii). One name which is notably absent is that of Lawrence Kersta (ibid.,

[3] The original version contained 96 chapters, but Solzhenitsyn did not envisage ever seeing it published and therefore created a second version which consisted of only 87 chapters. The German translation is based on this version. The full version was published in Moscow in 1991.

[4] This can be taken to refer to Koenig et al. [21], which contains a technical description of the Sound Spectrograph.

p.viii). While we do know from Kersta [15] that he indeed worked for Bell Laboratories at the time and was involved in extending the spectrograph, he is neither listed by Potter et al. ([30], p. viii) as being among those who developed the sound spectrograph nor as a member of the translator development team, let alone as a supervisor. His personal merit in the context of sound spectrography obviously consisted of expanding the methodology to display amplitudes [15] including the development a new kind of visualization, i.e., the "contour spectrogram (voiceprint)", in which amplitude "is shown by seven quantized or contour steps" ([16], p.1254). Its use in voice comparison is mentioned in the famous article in *Nature*, but the results for "contour type voiceprints" were in fact slightly worse than those of "bar type voiceprints" (ibid., p.1256).

According to Tosi ([39], p.415), Lawrence Kersta took up the idea of using sound spectrography for speaker identification purposes "at the request of a law enforcement group." In 1962, he published an article and two abstracts in highly reputed Journals, which set off an unfortunate development in forensic speaker identification [16; 17; 18]. These articles established the infamous analogy between voiceprints and fingerprints. Interestingly, his article published in *Nature* [16] does not contain any references to back up his ideas, but relies on personal convictions instead: "My claim to voice pattern uniqueness then rests on the improbability that two speakers would have vocal cavity dimensions and articulator use-patterns identical enough to confound voiceprint identification methods."(p.1255). He goes on to make a strong, yet unsubstantiated claim: "It is my opinion, however, that identifiable uniqueness does exist in each voice, and that masking, disguising, or distorting the voice will not defeat identification, if the speech is intelligible" ([16], p.1257). Kersta even went so far as to use ten words in voice comparison in order to emphasize the fingerprint analogy (ibid., p.1255). The closed-set experiments which he published seemed to support his claim of "voiceprint infallibility". In 1966, Kersta left Bell Labs and founded his own company called "Voiceprint Laboratories Corporation" in Somerville, N.J. ([25], p.87).

It is interesting to note that at that time the support by Bell Labs for the notion of voiceprints seems to have had receded to some extent. An internal report of June 1962 [3] is phrased much more carefully than Kersta's own publications: "He [i.e. Mr. Kersta, AB] believes that voice identification will eventually achieve a degree of accuracy somewhere between the present accuracy of identification by fingerprints and identification by handwriting" (p.215). The allusion to handwriting is most notable at this point in time – it reflects the observation made by Potter 17 years earlier (cf. 3.1 above). One might speculate that by that time the fingerprint analogy had been given up by those who had originally created it but was upheld by Kersta.

5.2 How voiceprints survived

In 1966, the first criminal case was tried in an American court in which voiceprint evidence was introduced (*People vs. Straehle* – a perjury case) with Lawrence Kersta as an expert. This trial resulted in a hung jury. According to Tosi ([40], pp.137f.), Kersta's company *Voiceprint Laboratories* worked on about 200 samples in total, but Kersta only ever testified eight times. Of those, voiceprints were admitted into evidence only once. The company went bankrupt in 1973. Lawrence Kersta passed away in 1994.

In 1970, the Michigan State Police established a *voice identification unit.* This unit worked on about 4,000 samples throughout the 1970s and testified in court about 65 times ([40], p.140). Of all samples, 3,400 (85%) were either eliminated from the process or resulted in a *non liquet*. Koenig ([20], p.2089) reports that "[t]he FBI conducts forensic voice identification examinations using the spectrographic or voiceprint technique for the FBI, other Federal agencies, state and local law enforcement authorities, and many foreign governments." He goes on to remark that those reports are "[...] for investigative support, but [the agents] have not provided expert court testimony on comparison results" ([20], p.2089). In other words, this method is deemed suitable for covert investigations by the FBI and for implicating, if not indicting, people, but the agents will not stand up to its results in court. Of the 2,000 comparisons reported by Koenig, about two thirds (65.2%) yielded a no decision or a low confidence decision. There were only 15.9% "identifications" ([20], p.2090). These numbers do not exactly speak for the practical usage of this method.

In the 1970s, ample evidence was published demonstrating the fallibility of voiceprint identification ([7; 11; 14], to name only a few). Hazen [11] found error rates of up to 52%, which are in sharp contrast to the 1% reported by Kersta ([16], p.1256). On a different strand, Tosi tried to render this procedure respectable by refuting the voiceprint analogy, adding auditory analysis and calling the method "aural and spectrographic examination" ([40], p. ix). In the late 1970s, voiceprint evidence was admissible in 23 states (ibid., p.143). The exact number of states whose judiciary will admit them today is not known to the present author, but voiceprint evidence continues to be used by the FBI (still without testifying to it, though; cf. [20]), and by some private companies, e.g., Owen Forensic Services LLC, run by Thomas Owen. What is worse, "[v]oice fingerprinting" is still considered to be the state-of-the-art technology in voice comparison in certain countries [27].

6 Conclusions

The perspective on *Visible Speech* has shifted from creating a tool for the training of the deaf towards a device depicting the major dimensions of speech: time, frequency, and intensity. While sound spectrograms have become an indispensable research tool which is used world-wide, they are totally unsuitable for the purposes which allegedly and actually led to their development in the first place in the US as well as the USSR, i.e. enabling the congenitally deaf to use the telephone as well as speaker identification. Sonagrams have indeed been used as models for training deaf persons to articulate more clearly, but in the past two decades, cochlear implants have become the method of choice. Whenever CIs did not turn out to be an option, spectrograms have been replaced by, e.g., ultrasound, because it reflects the actual tongue position more directly than the spectrogram.

As far as the forensic perspective is concerned, no properly qualified forensic phonetician would today subscribe to the analogy between spectrograms and fingerprints. The main reason for the latter is what Francis Nolan has termed the "plasticity of the vocal tract" ([26], p. 748], i.e. the inherent intraspeaker variability owing to age, health status, speaking context etc. which may well exceed interspeaker differences as are displayed in a spectrogram. And yet, the concept of voiceprints still seems so attractive to interested parties that it has not to date been eradicated.

Acknowledgements

I would like to thank Natalia Filatkina of the University of Trier for her kind assistance with the translation of the Russian original. I am indebted to Rebecca Nadolny of Nokia Bell Labs for her patient search for the Gray and Kopp Report and to Harry L. Harting for going through numerous microfilms at NARA trying to find that same document.

References:

[1] Abercrombie, David: Elements of General Phonetics. Edinburgh: Edinburgh University Press 1967.

[2] Amman, John Conrade: The Talking Deaf Man: A Method Proposed, Whereby He Who is Born Deaf, May Learn to Speak. Amsterdam: Westein 1692.

[3] Anon.: Voice Spectrograms Are Unique Personal Identification. Bell Laboratories Record, June 1962, 214-215.

[4] Baken, R.J.: Clinical Measurement of Speech and Voice. London: Taylor & Francis 1987.

[5] Baken, R.J. / Daniloff, R.G. (eds.): Readings in Clinical Spectrography of Speech. San Diego/Pine Brook, N.J.: Singular and Kay Elemetrics 1991.

[6] Bell, Alexander M.: Visible Speech: The Science of Universal Alphabetics; or self-interpreting Physiological Letters for the Writing of all Languages in one Alphabet. London /New York: N. Trübner & Co. 1867.

[7] Bolt, R. H. / Cooper, F. S. / Green, D. M. / Hamlet, S. L. / Hogan, D. L. / McKnight, J. G. / Pickett, J. M. / Tosi, O. / Underwood, B. D.: On the Theory and Practice of Voice Identification. Washington, D.C.: National Academy of Sciences 1979.

[8] Dudley, Homer / Gruenz, Otto O, Jr. (1946): Visible Speech Translators with External Phosphors. The Journal of the Acoustical Society of America 18 (1946), 62-73.

[9] Eriksson, A. (n.dat): Tutorial on *Forensic Speech Science.* 14p.

[10] Gray, C.H. / Kopp, G.A.: Voiceprint Identification. Bell Telephone Laboratories Report 1944, 1-14.

[11] Hazen, B.: Effects of differing phonetic contexts on spectrographic speaker identification. The Journal of the Acoustical Society of America 54 (1973), 650-660.

[12] Holder, William: Elements of Speech: An Essay of Inquiry into the Natural Production of Letters' with an Appendix concerning persons Deaf & Dumb. London 1669.

[13] Hollien, H.: The Acoustics of Crime. The new Science of Forensic Phonetics. New York etc. Plenum Press 1990.

[14] Hollien, H. / McGlone, R. E.: An evaluation of the "Voiceprint" technique of speaker identification. Proceedings of the Carnahan Conference on Crime Countermeasures. University of Kentucky: University of Kentucky Press, Lexington (1976), 39-45.

[15] Kersta, L.G.: Amplitude Cross-Section Representation with the Sound Spectrograph. The Journal of the Acoustical Society of America 20 (1948), 796-801

[16] Kersta, L. G.: Voiceprint Identification. Nature 196 (1962), 1253-1257.

[17] Kersta, L. G.: Voiceprint Identification. The Journal of the Acoustical Society of America 34 (1962), 725.

[18] Kersta, L. G.: Voiceprint Identification Infallibility. The Journal of the Acoustical Society of America 34 (1962), 1978.

[19] Kopp, G.A. / Green, H.C.: Basic Phonetic Principles of Visible Speech. The Journal of the Acoustical Society of America 18 (1946), 74-89.

[20] Koenig, B. E.: Spectrographic voice identification: A forensic survey. The Journal of the Acoustical Society of America 79 (1986), 2088-2090.

[21] Koenig, W. / Dunn, H.K. / Lacy, L.Y.: The Sound Spectrograph. The Journal of the Acoustical Society of America 18 (1946), 19-49.

[22] Künzel, H. J.: Sprechererkennung. Grundzüge forensischer Sprachverarbeitung. Heidelberg: Kriminalistik Verlag 1987.

[23] Lieberman, Philip / Blumstein, Sheila E.: Speech physiology, speech perception, and acoustic phonetics. Cambridge etc.: Cambridge University Press 1988.
[24] Lindh, J.: Handling the "Voiceprint" Issue. Proceedings FONETIK, Dept. of Linguistics, Stockholm University 2004, 4p.
[25] Meuwly, Didier: Reconnaissance de locuteurs en sciences forensiques: l'apport d'une approche automatique. Thèse de doctorat, Université de Lausanne 2001.
[26] Nolan, F.: Speaker Recognition and Forensic Phonetics. In: Hardcastle, J. and Laver, J. (eds.): The Handbook of Phonetic Sciences. Oxford etc.: Blackwell 1997, 744-767.
[27] Pragnesh, Parmar / Udhayabanu, R. : Voice Fingerprinting: A Very Important Tool against Crime. Journal of Indian Academy of Forensic Medicine 34 (2012), 70-73.
[28] Potter, R.K.: Visible Patterns of Sound. Science 102 (1945), 463-470.
[29] Potter, R.K.: Introduction to Technical Discussions of Sound Portrayal. The Journal of the Acoustical Society of America 18 (1946), 1-3.
[30] Potter, Ralph K. / Kopp, George A. / Green Kopp, Harriet: Visible Speech. New – York: Dover Publications 1947.
[31] Riesz, R.R. / Schott, L.: The Visible Speech Cathode-Ray Translator. The Journal of the Acoustical Society of America 18 (1946), 50-61.
[32] Rose, Philip: Forensic Speaker Identification. London/New York: Taylor & Francis 2002.
[33] Schubert, Hans: Historie der Schallaufzeichnung. Frankfurt am Main: Deutsches Rundfunkarchiv 2002.
[34] Smrkovski, Lonnie L.: Voice Identification. Michigan Department of State Police 1977.
[35] Solschenitsyn, Alexander: Der erste Kreis der Hölle. Frankfurt: S. Fischer 1968.
[36] Солженицын, А.И.: В круге первом. Москва: Панорама 1991.
[37] Steinberg, John C.: Application of Sound Measuring Instruments to the Study of Phonetic Problems. The Journal of the Acoustical Society of America VI (1934), 16-24.
[38] Steinberg, J.C. / French, N.R.: The Portrayal of Visible Speech. The Journal of the Acoustical Society of America 18 (1946), 4-18.
[39] Tosi, Oscar: The Problem of Speaker Identification and Elimination. In: Singh, Sadanand (ed.): Measurement Procedures in Speech, Hearing, and Language. Baltimore etc: University Park Press (1975), 399-431.
[40] Tosi, Oscar: Voice Identification. Theory and Legal Applications. Baltimore etc: University Park Press 1979.
[41] Wallis, John: Grammatica Linguae Anglicanae [with an appendix: De loquela, sive sonorum formatione, tractus grammatico-physicus.] London: Leon Lichfield 1653.

Music, notation and the representation of lexical tone

Murray Schellenberg
University of British Columbia, Canada
mhschellenberg@gmail.com

Abstract: Music has played a significant role in the study and analysis of lexical tone. This paper presents a brief summary of some of the ways scholars have used and adapted conventions of Western musical notation to further their study of tone. It also examines the possible influence of cultural perceptions of melody on Western perspectives of tone.

1 Introduction

Western scholars have been aware of tone languages at least since the early 1600s [12]. Since that time, missionaries and scientists have devised a wide range of systems to describe and express these tones on paper. Music has played a central role in the way that Western scholars have described and understood lexical tone. Tone languages have long been associated with music in the West, with lexical tones frequently been equated with music in academic discussions of tone languages. For example, Crowther [8, p.3] describes Yoruba as "very musical"; Douglas [10, p. 33] says that Chinese tones "partake of the nature of musical intonations"; Werner [24] and Haupt [14] both use the term "musical accent" as an equivalent for "tone"; and Davis [9, p. 154] describes Navaho as "a singing language". Cognitive scientists have also linked linguistic tones and musical pitch in cognitive processing (e.g. [16], [11]).

Early European scholars who wished to express lexical tones in writing faced a challenge. Western European orthographies represent speech sounds but they don't represent the changes in pitch that characterize the speech act. However, when early scholars wanted to express pitch in language they had at hand a system that was designed expressly to represent both pitch and rhythm: musical notation.

This paper is not intended as an in depth discussion of all the various ways that tones have been described or annotated. Rather, the aim is to lay out a brief history of the diversity and potential usefulness of music-based tone/pitch annotation in speech. This paper will explore some of the ways in which the Western view of and approach to music have had an influence on the ways in which scholars from that same society have portrayed pitch in language. While the primary focus will be on the representation of linguistic tone, many of the same influences may also be found in other areas such as intonation. It should also be noted that both music and tone also involve duration as well as pitch and that representations of duration can be found in many of the descriptions described in this paper. For reasons of brevity, however, the discussion in this paper will be limited solely to pitch.

Section 2 will present a very brief resumé of the development of musical notation in Western Europe; sometimes referred to as the first technology for capturing pitch in the West [15]. The subsequent sections will introduce different ways that scholars have used Western musical notation to represent lexical tones; starting with attempts to transcribe speech tones directly into musical notation and moving through various adaptations that have been used. The final section gives a brief discussion of the idea of melody as a cultural construction and offers some suggestions on how the prevailing Western European conception of melody may have had an influence on the academic interpretation of lexical tones.

Figure 1. Example of neumes from 11th century manuscript. The neumes are written over the words for the antiphon *Non turbetur. St. Gallen, Stiftsbibliothek, Codex Sangallensis 387, p. 144 (excerpt) – Breviary, summer portion (with neumes)*

2 Western Musical Notation – A system for capturing sound

Sound is ephemeral – once it is made, it disappears completely. For thousands of years the only way to reproduce a sound was to remember it and then to make it again. Writing was the first technology for recording sound with written language long predating written music in the West [15, 21]. The earliest songbooks in medieval Europe were just books of words used for the many religious services in monasteries. Monks spent a good portion of their day chanting – and the chants were often different from one day to the next. Without a system for notating the melodies, the only way for the monks to learn the melody for a particular chant was to hear it and then try to remember it [15]. While some chants were repeated fairly frequently, others were sung only once a year or even less often. At some point, a monk with a poor memory (probably various monks in different places) started to write in reminders of the melody above the words in the songbook. Soon these reminders were being copied into new books that were being produced. Figure 1 shows an example of this kind of notation from a breviary (book of liturgical texts) produced at the Abbey of St. Gall in Switzerland between 1022 and 1047. This early notation consists of lines, dots and squiggles (collectively called neumes) that give indications of how the melody moves. As the words were already written from left to right, the music notation acquired the same left-to-right alignment. Pitch level within a neume was indicated via higher pitches being closer to the top of the page. Sometimes the relative pitch level of adjacent neumes was indicated by vertical placement on the page … but often it wasn't [15].

The neumes, it is important to note, served only as reminders of a melody already known. Someone who didn't know the melody would not be able to reconstruct what it should sound like by reading the neumes. If you wanted to learn it, you still had to find someone who already knew the melody to teach it to you.

That changed thanks to a man called Guido d'Arezzo, a Tuscan monk who lived from around 995 to about 1050 [18]. Somewhere around 1030 Guido devised – or at least, wrote down – a new system for recording music. This system involved drawing a grid of 4 horizontal lines and superimposing the neumes on it. Grid lines had been used prior to this [12] but Guido's real innovation was to specify that any neume written on a particular line or space of the grid would always have the same (relative) pitch. He also specified the relationships between the pitches – the distance between adjacent notes is not always the same [15]. His pitch relationships are still used today as our modern day major scale and his gridlines were the forerunner to the modern musical staff. This innovation led to a major change in the usability of musical notation: it now became possible for someone who had never heard a song before to learn it without a teacher [15]. An example of this type of notation from a 15th century Italian gradual (book with the music for the mass) is shown in figure 2. Over time, musicians

Figure 2. Music with fixed relative pitches on a 4-line staff. Excerpt from Alleluia for mass on Christmas Day – 15th century Italian manuscript. *UBC, Italian 15th century gradual [M]. http://dx.doi.org/10.14288/1.0054703*

have made further refinements to the system but the basic 5-line staff and pitch relationships of notes used by musicians today have their direct antecedents in the innovations of Guido d'Arezzo.

3 Using Musical Staff Notation for Tone

Remarkably few scholars have used the Western musical notation system directly to represent lexical tones but it has been done. This section presents two examples: one from a description of Thai in the mid-nineteenth century and one from a Mandarin grammar from the 1960s.

The first example is the 1850 grammar of Thai [20] written (in Latin) by Denis Jean Baptiste Pallegoix who was the Bishop of Siam (as it was then called). The chapter on tone is brief (8 pages in a book of 241 pages) but in it, he provides typographic representations of the tones via accent markings. He also (p. 36) provides musical transcriptions of not only the tones in isolation (as shown in figure 3) but also provides (loc. cit.) musical transcriptions of very brief samples of colloquial speech (*modulus in colloquio communi*), prose recitation (*in recitation prosœ*), preaching (*in prœdicatione*) and singing (*in recitatione carminum*). Pallegoix's transcriptions would have to have been made based on his own perceptions of native speakers. They are somewhat different from the modern-day representation of the Thai tone contours (c.f. figure 9, for example) but certainly express distinct differences. They would also have been easily perceived and produced by anyone able to read music.

The second example comes from Yuen Ren Chao in his 1965 *Grammar of Spoken Chinese* [7]. In addition to written descriptions of the tones and their representation in the IPA tone letters (see 5.1 below), Chao provides a brief representation of the tones transcribed musically (Figure 4). Western descriptions of Mandarin tones have assigned numbers to the four tones and Chao presents the tones in that numerical order. Unlike Pallegoix, Chao does not provide sample words beneath the tones but presents the musical score independent of the words.

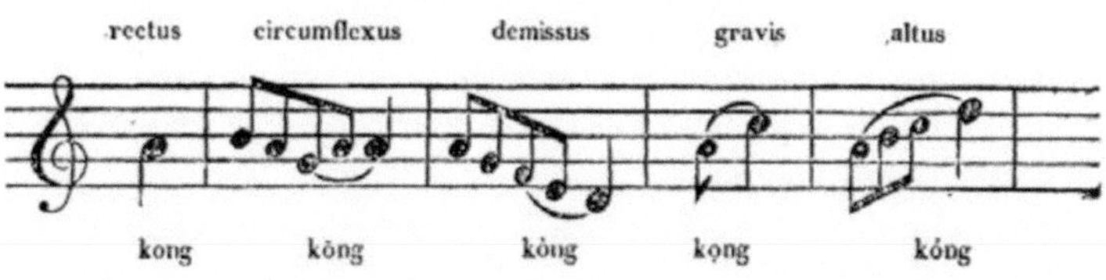

Figure 3. Musical notation used to explain tone in Thai. The typographic tone marks can be seen on the vowels of the words under the score [20, p. 36]

Figure 4. Musical notation used to explain tone in Mandarin [7, p. 26]

It is interesting that Chao – who is as renowned a composer as he is a linguist – chose to add musical notation at a time when other graphic representations such as pitch contour graphs were also readily available. This choice probably reflects what is one of the major advantages of using musical notation: it is a very widely understood system. It is immediately accessible to a wide range of people and has such a common base of understanding that it takes little to no explanation for a very large proportion of people to get a clear picture of both the pitch contours and relative pitch levels.

Music notation, however, is not necessarily very accurate for the representation of speech. Pitch and melody in (Western) music are not really the same as pitch and melody in speech. In 1779, Steele [22] noted that:

> [Music is] a series of sounds moving distinctly from grave to acute, or vice versa (either gradually or *saltim*) by intervals, of which the semi tone (commonly so called) may be the common measure or divisor, without a fraction, and always dwelling, for a perceptible space of time, on one certain tone.
>
> Whereas the melody of speech moves rapidly up or down by slides, wherein no graduated distinction of tones or semitones can be measured by the ear; nor does the voice (in our language) ever dwell distinctly, for any perceptible space of time, on any certain level or uniform tone, except the last tone on which the speaker ends or makes a pause. (p. 4)

Steele [22] was just one of the scholars who decided to take standard musical notation and modify it to make it more useful for depicting pitch in speech.

4 Modifications of Staff Notation

In his 1779 book, *Prosodia Rationalis: Or, An Essay Towards Establishing The Melody And Measure Of Speech, To Be Expressed And Perpetuated By Peculiar Symbols*, Joshua Steele lays out a system to notate the prosody of speech so writers and orators could notate the prosodic component of speech. While his system was not intended to be used for tone languages it is worth noting in the context of tonal representations as he takes the syllable as the basic unit for pitch notation and notates contours for each syllable.

Significantly, Steele explicitly chose to make his system a modification of the Western musical notation system. He explains [22, p. 8] that he decided to develop a system "which might come as near as possible to the modern notation of music, in order to make it the easier to be comprehended by those whose ideas of sounds and measure of time are already formed on that plan." But he needed to find a way to express the "slides" of speech which exhibited "no gradual distinction of tones" [22, p.4].

An example of his notation is given in figure 5. His system is based on the 5-line staff of modern music notation, but each space between the lines is further subdivided to provide a line for each semitone in the Western scale. The pitch contour of each syllable is drawn as a dark line and the various tails attached to each contour indicate different rhythms (the calli-

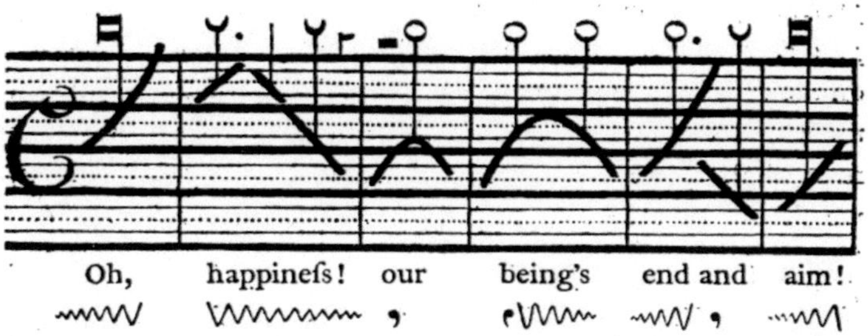

Figure 5. Example of Steele's proposed speech prosody notation [22, p. 13]

graphic C at the beginning is a time signature). The sinusoidal lines and commas below the words indicate amplitude variation.

Over a century later, in the 1930s, Douglas Beach devised a very similar system (described in [23]) of expanding the standard 5-line staff to produce a massive 29-line staff to encompass a pitch range of an octave and a third (figure 6b). It is interesting to note that his subdivisions of the original 5-line staff precisely matches that of Steele with the outer spaces of the staff being subdivided into four and the inner spaces being subdivided into three (see figure 6) Beach added a further 7 lines above and 7 lines below. Tucker [23, p.596], who was a student of Beach, relates that "students, armed with tuning-forks, were set to record on these sheets accurate representations of tones as heard from phonograph cylinders, picking the needle up at each syllable."

These expanded staves provide a somewhat finer representation of pitch than the conventional staff notation of music. As each line represents a semitone, it is possible to notate pitch down to quarter tones by using the space between the lines to indicate the space between the notes [22, p.5]. The density of the lines, however, makes rapid reading much more difficult. Both Steele and Beach tried to alleviate this somewhat by changing the density and pattern of the lines but it is still difficult to read quickly. It is possible, for example, to determine that the rise on the first syllable in Figure 5 is 15 semitones – but only after careful counting. Determining accurate pitch changes quickly is tricky.

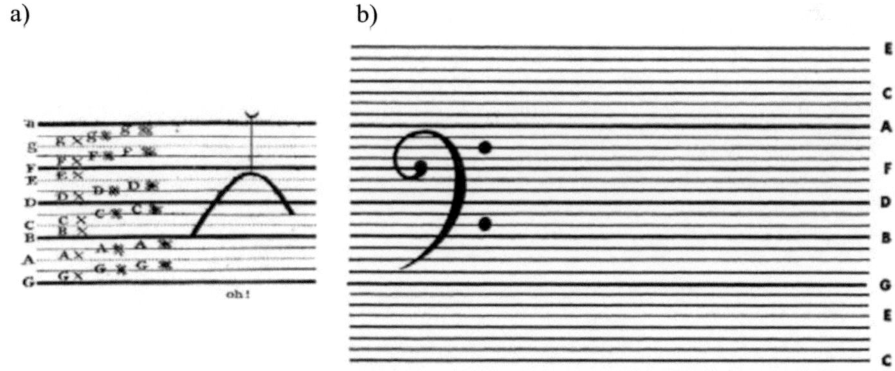

Figure 6. Comparison of expanded staves used by (a) Steele [22, p. 5] and (b) Beach [23, p. 596]

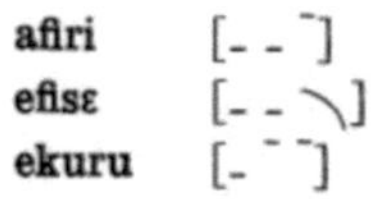

Figure 7. Ward's diagrammatic system for 3 words in Twi (as shown in [23])

5 Staffless Pictorial Representations

As absolute pitch is not generally necessary for depictions of tone, pictorial representations of tone have often abandoned the musical staff. The traditions of Western music, however, have had various influences on these representations, as well. For example, all of the systems discussed below (and many others, as well) mirror two of the most basic conventions of musical notation: time is portrayed along the horizontal axis from left to right and pitch is portrayed along the vertical axis with higher pitches being shown as closer to the top of the page. As well, scholars have regularly employed musical note names and musical intervals to express pitch levels and ranges.

5.1 Diagrammatic systems accompanying orthography

The tone letters used as part of the International Phonetic Alphabet were first suggested in an article by Yuen Ren Chao in 1930 [6]. The letters consist of a vertical line divided into 4 equal parts, thus providing 5 numbered points. A "time-pitch curve" is drawn to the left of the line indicating the shape and pitch level(s) of the syllable's tone (e.g. ˥˧, ˩˧). The musical influences are not, perhaps, as readily apparent from the symbols but the time-pitch curves very definitely mimic the time/pitch relationship of musical notation. Furthermore, the divisions on the vertical line are based on musical intervals. Chao [6, p. 25] stipulates that "each step may be taken to be a whole tone, thus making the total equal to an augmented fifth." The divisions of tone steps in this system are equated directly to musical intervals.

Another pictorial system uses dashes and lines to express tone movement in language (see Figure 7). Ida Ward made extensive use of one such system in a series of African language primers in the 1930s [23]. This system involved using vertically positioned dashes to indicate pitch height and curves to indicate rises or falls.

Tucker [23, p. 600] describes it as "an eminently pedagogic system, and not intended for indigenous authors; but she [*Ward*] felt that the Westermann system [*an orthographic system of accent marks*] lacked sufficient tone marks for the necessary levels of down step which she had to teach. Her system's main disadvantage was its expense, though the English printers were very accommodating and allowed her five levels of horizontal line per block." The resulting tone descriptions look remarkably like the neumes in the hymn books of the medieval monks (Figure 1).

Figure 8. Caswell's 1870 diagram of Thai tones. [5, p. 95]. He describes Thai as having only 4 tones (C, D, E and F). The line AB is the "pitch of the voice in reading English"

5.2 Pitch contours

The tradition of horizontal time and vertical pitch are also found in the linear pitch contours, a representation frequently used to portray tones today. Figure 8 shows an early diagram of this sort from 1870 [5]. This is another description of the tones of Thai. Caswell [5] describes Thai as having only 4 tones (conflating the two level tones). His description runs "Let the line AB represent the natural key, or pitch of the voice in reading English … C will represent the rising inflection, D the falling inflection, E the depressed tone, and F the circumflex tone." [5, p. 95]. He uses the idea of a reference line not dissimilar to a musical staff line around which he can arrange pictorial descriptions of the four tones.

The influence of music continued with the advent of mechanical means of recording pitch. Cornelius Bradley was the first to use the kymograph to record the production of tones [4]; first in Thai [2] and then in Cantonese and Mandarin [3]. In 1916 he published a monograph explaining the procedures he used to produce his pitch contours [4]. The kymograph was used to record the waveforms of the tones; fundamental frequency values were then computed from hand measurements taken off the waveform and subsequently graphed. Figure 9 shows his 1911 graph of the tones for Thai [2]. Note that the pitches are given as musical note equivalents along the vertical axis despite the measurements all having been made in cycles per second. Musical notes are still an easy and convenient way of making pitch values accessible.

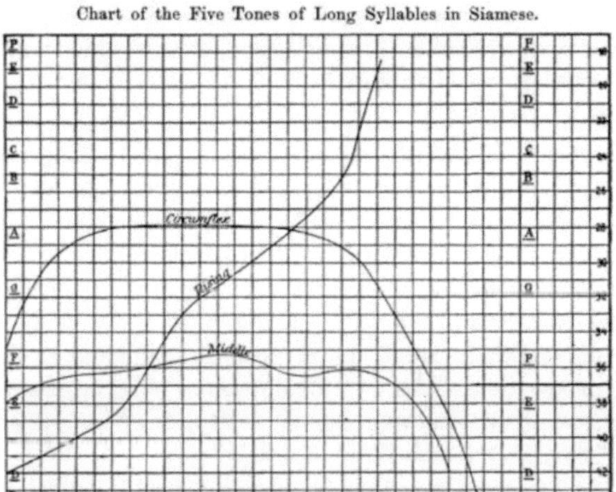

Figure 9. Bradley's pitch contours of Thai Tones based on kymographic recordings [2]

6 Pitch and the Conception of Melody

The preceding examples have all shown ways in which the system of musical notation prevalent in the West has influenced, to varying degrees, visual representations of pitch (primarily tone) in language. This section takes a somewhat more ethnomusicological approach and attempts to look at what influence the culturally specific Western-European conception of melody has had on the perception of tone by scholars from that culture.

Any musical system is a cultural construct which has modified and molded the auditory signal in ways that reflect what that culture deems to be important. Nettl [19, p. 85] points out that "there may be, in certain cultures, segments of sound more significant than those we label as 'notes'". Ethnomusicologists have wrestled for years with the difficulty of defining music and describing, for a primarily Western audience, non-Western conceptions of music [19]. While a given acoustic signal may be non-cultural, its perception by an individual is highly coloured by cultural factors [19, 21] – which have been described as "norms determined by the vast aggregate of practice and codified by generations of workers" [21, p. 193]. While Seeger in that description is referring specifically to notation, his description applies equally well to the development of any cultural norm.

The conception of melody is an excellent example of something that is open to cultural interpretation. Seeger [21] proposes that melody is something that may be conceived in a variety of ways. He suggests that "on one hand ... melody may be conceived ... as a succession of separate sounds, on the other, as a single continuum of sound" (p. 185). He further divides the conception of melody as a continuum into two different possibilities: "as a chain or as a stream. Conception as a chain tends to emphasize structure and entities that move; conception as a stream, function and movement" (p. 185).

The concept of melody in the West is, of course, very much a conception of discrete units in a sequence. This can be seen in the very idea of musical "notes" so prevalent in the music of Europe and North America. The early development of neumes into representations of individuated pitches suggests that Western cultures have long conceived melody as consisting of discreet pitch units.

The Western conception of melody as a series of individual pitch targets has interesting implications for our understanding of how we perceive pitch and melody in speech. Lexical tones, for example, are theoretically conceived in Western linguistics as discrete pitch units: high and low. It is possible to see the idea of lexical tones as pitch targets as being influenced (perhaps unintentionally) by the prevailing musical conceptions of melody and pitch. Did we simply transfer over our musical perceptions to language?

While this perception/construction of tone has allowed the development of extremely useful insights into language it is not the only way to conceive of tone. Chinese scholars at the time of Middle Chinese (roughly 420 – 1273 C.E.) categorized the tones of Middle Chinese as level, rising, departing and entering [1, 16]. Mei [17, p.91ff] provides a fascinating translation of a 7th century Japanese description of these four Chinese tones:

> The level tone was level and low, with both the light and the heavy; the rising tone was level and high, with only the light but not the heavy; the departing tone was slightly drawn out, with no [distinction between] the light and the heavy; the entering tone stops abruptly, having neither the inner nor the outer; the level tone [carried by syllables] with nasal or lateral initials was indistinguishable from the heavy; and the heavy of the rising tone was no different from the departing tone. (*annotations from* [17])

While an in-depth discussion of the Middle Chinese tone system is well beyond the scope of this paper, it is interesting to note that the names of the tones (albeit in translation) appear to have an emphasis on movement and contour and not on pitch height. Scholars interested in tone in Middle Chinese appear to have been more influenced by poetry than music [1, 16] and their approach to categorizing tones is quite different to that of modern Western scholars.

7 Conclusion

Music has had a continuing influence on how Western scholars represent lexical tones. Although musical notation itself acquired some of its conventions from language (primarily the left-to-right use of the page), conventions of musical notation such as pitch height being towards the top of the page have become standard in pictorial depictions of lexical tone. The widespread use of musical notation culturally has meant that use of this notation has made representations of lexical tone easily accessible and understandable to a population that does not speak a tone language. However, the differences between speech and music have meant that adaptations have often been desirable. Scholars have adapted musical notation in various ways but its conventions have often prevailed. Even when tone notation systems have appeared to be quite different from music notation, scholars have often relied on musical note names and pitch intervals to make their work more readily accessible and understandable.

As well, the Western European construction of melody as a series of individual notes has possibly also been influential in the prevailing idea of lexical tone being constructed of individual units. As mentioned before, this has led to many fascinating insights but it is possible that additional insights might be made by reconceiving tones in a "movement" conception.

This paper has tried to show that music has had a regular and important influence on Western linguistic research into lexical tones. Musical notation has provided a ready means by which scholars have been able to record and preserve sound and make it available to others. Often this influence has gone unrecognized but awareness of these connections may allow future scholars to bring new insights to the field.

8 References

[1] BAXTER, W. H.: *A handbook of Old Chinese phonology*. Walter de Gruyter. 1992.

[2] BRADLEY, C. B.: *Graphic analysis of the tone-accents of the Siamese language. Journal of the American Oriental Society*, vol. 31, no. 3, pp. 282-289, 1911.

[3] BRADLEY, C. B.: *The tone-accents of two Chinese dialects. Journal of the American Oriental Society*, vol. 35, pp. 199-206, 1915

[4] BRADLEY, C. B.: *On plotting the inflections of the voice*. University of California Press, 1916.

[5] CASWELL, J.: *Treatise on the tones of the Siamese language*. In SMITH S. J. (ed.): *Siam repository*, vol. 2, no. 1, pp. 93-101, 1870.

[6] CHAO, Y. R.: *A system of tone letters. Le Maître Phonetique*, vol. 45. pp. 24-27, 1930.

[7] CHAO, Y. R.: *A grammar of spoken Chinese*. University of California Press, 1965.

[8] CROWTHER, S.: *A grammar of the Yoruba language*. Seeleys, 1852.

[9] DAVIS, E. C.: *New written language makes debut in America. The Science News-letter*, vol. 37, no.10, pp. 154-157, 1940.

[10] DOUGLAS, R. K.: *The language and literature of China*. London: Trübner & Co, 1875.

[11] GIULIANO, R. J., PFORDRESHER, P. Q., STANLEY, E. M., NARAYANA, S., & WICHA, N. Y.: *Native experience with a tone language enhances pitch discrimination and the timing of neural responses to pitch change. The Relationship between Music and Language*, vol. 14, 2011.

[12] HAIR, P. E. H.: *A nineteenth-century link between Chinese and African language studies. Bulletin of the School of Oriental and African Studies*, vol. 29, no.1, pp. 143-145, 1966.

[13] HAINES, J.: *The origins of the musical staff. The Musical Quarterly*, vol. 91, no. 3-4, pp.327-378, 2009.

[14] HAUPT, P.: *Tones in Sumerian. Journal of the American Oriental Society*, vol. 37, pp. 309-323, 1917.

[15] KELLY, T. F.: *Capturing music: The story of notation*. W.W. Norton & Company, 2014.

[16] KRISHNAN, A., XU, Y., GANDOUR, J., & CARIANI, P.: *Encoding of pitch in the human brainstem is sensitive to language experience. Cognitive Brain Research*, vol. 25, no. 1, pp. 161-168, 2005.

[17] MEI, TSU-LIN.: *Tones and prosody in Middle Chinese and the origin of the rising tone. Harvard Journal of Asiatic Studies*, vol. 30, pp. 86-110, 1970.

[18] MILLER, S. D.: Guido d'Arezzo: *Medieval musician and educator. Journal of Research in Music Education*, vol. 21, no. 3, pp. 239-245, 1973.

[19] NETTL, B.: *The study of ethnomusicology: Thirty-one issues and concepts*. University of Illinois Press, 2010.

[20] PALLEGOIX, J. B.: *Grammatica linguae Thai*. Bangkok: Collegii Assumptionis, 1850

[21] SEEGER, C.: *Prescriptive and descriptive music-writing. The Musical Quarterly*, vol. 44, no. 2, 184-195, 1958.

[22] STEELE, J.: *Prosodia rationalis: or, an essay towards establishing the melody and measure of speech, to be expressed and perpetuated by peculiar symbols*. London: J. Nichols, 1779

[23] TUCKER, A. N.: *Systems of tone-marking African languages. Bulletin of the School of Oriental and African Studies*, vol. 27, no. 3, pp. 594-611, 1964.

[24] WERNER, A. *Language and folklore in West Africa. Journal of the African Society*, vol. 6, no. 21, 65-83, 1906.

On the History of Computational Modelling and Simulations in the Phonetic Sciences

Daniel Duran

University of Stuttgart, Germany
daniel.duran@ims.uni-stuttgart.de

Abstract: This paper presents a study on the history of simulation studies in phonetics. Precursors to modern computational models are identified in early mechanical speaking machines. By way of illustration, the historical development is analysed as documented in the proceedings of the International Congress of Phonetic Sciences from 1932 to 2015.

1 Introduction

State of the art methods of computational modelling and simulations in phonetics and phonology have their roots, a.o., in early work on mechanical *speaking machines*. It is less widely known, that numerical simulations with digital computers also have a relatively long history in the speech sciences. In order to understand the history of the application of computational modelling techniques and simulations in phonetics and phonology, a broader perspective is necessary. The advancements of simulation studies within other scientific fields, such as computational linguistics, artificial intelligence, psychology, cognitive and social science are important. As are those advancements in methodology in speech and natural language processing. Simulations entered the fields of phonetics and phonology from different directions. Phonetics is most closely connected with speech synthesis and artificial speech recognition. Phonology, on the other hand, is closely connected with modelling in (computational) linguistics.

Two kinds of research are often discussed with respect to *methodology* in phonetic sciences: Field work, which observes its subject of study *in situ*, and experimental or laboratory work, which could be said to study language *in vitro*. Both observe language and speech *in vivo*, i.e. on living, speaking humans. This paper is concerned with a different kind of research method that emerged during the past six decades: the study of language and speech by means of computational modelling and simulations, observing the subject of study *in silico*. At the 1995 ICPhS in Stockholm, Roger K. Moore presented a "trigger paper" in which he argues for a new, unified research discipline, "*Computational Phonetics*", which addresses speech production and perception by both humans and machines [1]. He notes that this new phonetic discipline is located at the intersection of various scientific disciplines: "Moreover it is precisely in the area of 'speech technology' [...] that the experimental and descriptive fields of phonetics, linguistics and psychology meet the computational disciplines of artificial intelligence, computer science and engineering" [1, p.68]. Moore points out that the progress in speech technology is primarily not due to the integration of linguistic knowledge but due to the application of rigorous mathematical and statistical methods and the increased available computational power [1, p.69]. Tillmann (at the same 1995 ICPhS) defines *Computational Phonetics* as follows: "[...] theories that take values of some given type and compute new values which are not trivially available in the computed form" [2].

It is not possible to provide a complete overview of the history of computational modelling in speech sciences, including phonetics and phonology. This paper discusses exemplary studies and reviews their contributions to the field. This paper may serve as a guide and starting point for further research on individual computational approaches and the development of the simulation methodology as a whole. In this paper I restrict myself to the discussion of the historical origins of computational approaches and computer simulations in phonetics which are not presented systematically in other reviews of the history of phonetics.

1.1 Historiography of phonetics and phonology

Koerner [3] provides a review of the historiography of phonetics. He points out that probably "the most thorough treatment of the history of phonetics to date" is the one provided in the second edition to Zwirner and Zwirner's *Grundfragen der Phonometrie*[1]. They [4] provide a detailed overview of phonetics as a philosophical and scientific treatment of spoken language. As far as methods are concerned, they mention Kempelen (see below). In plenary talks at the 12th ICPhS, Liénard [5] reviews the developments from speaking machines to speech synthesis, and Stevens [6] reviews the influence of Klatt's speech synthesizer on phonetics. A detailed overview of the history of speech synthesis – probably the most detailed one – is provided by Köster [7]. An equally thorough treatment of the history of simulations in phonetics and phonology is still missing. Loakes [8] gives an overview of the history of experimental phonetics. She points out important "tools" in phonetics: the International Phonetic Alphabet (IPA) for transcriptions and software packages like Praat and EMU for acoustic analysis. She notes that "it is really the advent of new technologies enabling phoneticians to answer vastly different types of questions about speech" [8, p.126f].

1.2 Terminology

For the purpose of this historical overview, it is first necessary to define some terminology. A *simulation* is defined here as a research technique or method of analysing a given system based on a model of that system. In this case *model* is intentionally ambiguous, referring to both an abstract, formal model as well as a physical simplified replica of a real world object or an apparatus. A model can be informally defined as a theoretical construct used to "explain something in the world" [9]. A *system* in that sense is any formal or real-world object with an internal structure or a set of connected, interacting elements.

A study employing methods from speech technology may be considered a phonetic simulation if the technology is not the focus but used as a research tool to investigate theories or models of human speech production, perception or processing. Fant [10, p.13], for example, notes: "Instead of speaking about phonetics and speech technology, we could make a distinction between theory and applications [...]". According to Fant's proposal, computer simulation studies in phonetics and phonology might thus be characterised as those studies which on the one hand employ computational modelling and methods of speech technology, but which on the other hand are not primarily concerned with applications.

2 Thought experiments and simulations

Far less well documented than the method of speech synthesis is the method of thought experiments as one root of computational simulation approaches. Thomason [11] discusses language acquisition and language change as two areas of linguistics in which the device of thought experiments is used by linguists. These are also two areas in which phonetic and phonological simulations are applied for the same reasons that Thomason [11, p.251] states: these areas are

[1] References in this present paper are made to the third, expanded edition, titled *Grundfragen der phonometrischen Linguistik* [4].

"hard to study by direct experimentation". Ohala [12] presents a thought experiment on the evolution of the primitive nature of the segment in phonology. He points out that a computational implementation "was not successful due to the enormity of the computations required and the need to define more carefully the concept of 'segmentality', the expected outcome". Note, however, that a "simple" computational simulation of a hypothetical vowel inventory is employed by Ohala [12] to demonstrate one aspect of his argument.

The ultimate *result* of a simulation is usually a hypothesis [13, p.599]. This is different from the *solution* which is calculated with a computational simulation, i.e. the solution of the underlying mathematical problem. One characteristic feature of computer simulations is that the model and the target system "are made of the same stuff" [13].

3 Rise of the Speaking machines

The artificial creation of speech sounds can be traced back to myths and anecdotal reports about speaking statues from ancient Egypt to the legendary talking head of Albertus Magnus in the 13th century. For the history of simulations in the phonetic sciences are such *speaking machines* of interest which were created out of scientific curiosity. Two traditions can be distinguished: the constructors of such machines tried to simulate the process of articulation and incorporated the available anatomical knowledge of their time. Alternatively, the machines were created with a primary interest in speech sounds without the intention to replicate human articulation.

The early mechanical speaking machines are closely related to musical instruments. The analogy of speech production with aerophones "makes sense from an articulatory point of view", as Fagyal [14] remarks: both produce sound by a (constricted) stream of air. She points out: "[...] 17th century inventors' knowledge about the mechanical reproduction of sounds had to come from musical instruments, because grammar books could not be of much use in this respect" [14]. Brackhane [15] points out the close relation between early mechanical speech synthesis and pipe organs (especially the *vox humana*). He describes how the *vox humana* has been idealised as a (supposedly) most natural imitation of the human voice and how this misconception probably lead to the prevailing approach of using is as a voice source in speech synthesis. The idea of a connection between organ-building and mechanical speech synthesis survived until the 20th century [15]. At the first ICPhS, for example, Paget [16] presented mechanical speech synthesis using an organ reed. He uses an organ reed to demonstrate that speech production involves two mechanisms: phonation and articulation. This is an example of a simulation which is used to test a hypothesis.

Historical sources suggest that working speaking machines may have been constructed even earlier than the 18th century [14, 7]. In the 1667 edition of *La Science Universelle*, a textbook on modern science by Charles Sorel, sieur de Souvigny, a hypothetical "speaking machine" is described as a musical instrument with pipes and a keyboard. Another source is Marin Mersenne's work *Harmonie Universelle, contenant la théorie et la pratique de la Musique* (1636) where he also wrote on speaking machines and reported on constructing an instrument to produce vowels. The sources of Sorel's "description of a semi-automatic, multilingual speaking machine modelled after a hydraulic organ, with the potential of using unlimited vocabulary" are traced to 17th century writings on science and mechanics. This suggests that the first attempts at constructing speaking machines were in fact made one century earlier than the documented constructions of the first speaking machines [14].

The beginning of scientific work on mechanical speech synthesis, however, can be identified with the seminal speaking machines by Kratzenstein, Abbé Mical and von Kempelen in the 18th century [17, 18, 19]. While the speaking machines by Kratzenstein or von Kempelen are widely recognised as early achievements in mechanical speech synthesis, the machines constructed by Abbé Mical are not generally known (as well as Mical himself).

By the end of the 18th century, mechanical speech synthesis has been introduced as a research method in the phonetic sciences, which has been further developed until early 20th century [7]. Today, mechanical models of the human vocal tract can still be found, for example, as teaching aids [cf. 20].

4 Systematic literature review of ICPhS proceedings

In this section I present the results of a systematic literature of ICPhS proceedings.

4.1 Quantitative Analysis

I adopt the following working definition of 'simulation study' and search criteria to conduct this literature review: A computer simulation in phonetics and phonology is a research method which involves one of the following:

- artificial speech production (synthesis)
- artificial speech recognition (ASR)
- interacting agents exchanging messages adhering to a given grammar
- formal languages in a dynamic system with external influence (e.g. noise)

A study employing methods from speech technology may be considered a phonetic simulation if

- the technology is not the focus but used as a research tool to investigate theories or models of human speech production, perception or processing

Does the use of synthetic speech stimuli constitute a phonetic simulation study? I leave this question open for discussion. [21], for example, investigate the perception of voice quality variations with synthesized speech samples. [22] present a method to synthesize pathological voice qualities and evaluate synthesized samples through perception tests. I omit papers on text-to-speech synthesis or automatic speech recognition which primarily focus on the technology. A rule of thumb could be this one: if both the *method* applied in a reported study as well as its *topic* are "speech synthesis", then it is probably a paper on speech technology and not a proper phonetic simulation study. As the proceedings of some congresses were not available electronically at the time of conducting this review, they have been reviewed in print. A complete search through the papers for relevant key-words was not possible due to time constraints. The total number of studies incorporating some form of simulations thus has to be seen as a conservative estimate.

4.2 Content Analysis

As a first approach (or, rather, as a methodological exercise) towards a qualitative analysis, the full texts of the relevant papers from the ICPhS proceedings can be analysed with methods from information retrieval and natural language processing. The analysis is restricted to papers identified as *relevant* for the history of computational modelling and simulations in phonetics as described in the previous section. As a further restriction, only papers written in English are included in the content analysis. All calculations have been performed in R using the *NLP*, *tidyverse* and *wordcloud* packages [23, 24, 25, 26]. Relevant papers from proceedings available

Table 1. Total number of contributions for selected ICPhS and the (estimated) number of contributions involving simulations ("sim."). Last two columns indicate the source (printed volumes or PDFs) and number of papers analysed (section 4.2). "NA" indicates missing data.

	congress	year	contributions			proceedings	analysed
			total	sim.	%		
1	Amsterdam	1932	62	1	1.61%	1 vol. print	0
2	London	1935	89	0	0.00%	1 vol. print	0
3	Ghent	1938	87	0	0.00%	1 vol. print	0
4	Helsinki	1961	102	6	5.88%	1 vol. print	4
5	Münster	1964	146	5	3.42%	1 vol. print	5
6	Prague	1967	238	1	0.42%	1 vol. print	1
7	Montréal	1971	162	6	3.70%	1 vol. print	3
8	Leeds	1975	NA	NA	NA	NA	0
9	Copenhagen	1979	250	9	3.60%	3 vol. print	2
10	Utrecht	1983	122	11	9.02%	1 vol. print	3
11	Tallin	1987	650	13	2.00%	5/6 vol. print	13
12	Aix-en-Provence	1991	562	25	4.45%	5 vol. print	25
13	Stockholm	1995	860	52	6.05%	4 vol. print	51
14	San Francisco	1999	642	24	3.74%	full PDF	24
15	Barcelona	2003	859	45	5.24%	full PDF	45
16	Saarbrücken	2007	533	31	5.82%	full PDF	31
17	Hong Kong	2011	579	15	2.59%	full PDF	15
18	Glasgow	2015	774	16	2.07%	full PDF	16

in print have been scanned and the text has been extracted automatically using OCR with some manual corrections.

In order to obtain a list of the most *specific* words for each year, the well-known *tf-idf* vector-space measure for document similarity [27] is used. This measure captures how central a specific word is to a document in comparison to other documents. It assigns a high score for terms which are frequent within one document (*term-frequency, tf*) but do not occur in many other documents (*inverse document frequency, idf*). For this analysis, all simulation-related papers from one congress are treated as a single "document" for which *tf-idf* scores are calculated. The tokens have been converted to all lower case.

4.3 Results

Table 1 shows an overview of the number of related contributions taken from ICPhS proceedings [28, 29, 30, 31, 32, 33, 34, 35, 36, 37, 38, 39, 40, 41, 42, 43]. The numbers from this quantitative analysis show that there is an increasing number of simulation studies. However, the relative proportion of studies including simulations is relatively low. Across all proceedings, 21 contributions contain the keyword "simulation" in their title and 73 in their abstract. 240 contributions refer to some form of "model" in their titles and 513 in their abstract. The adjusted number of contributions presenting studies which applied the method of computational modelling and simulations as defined in this present paper is given in column "sim." of Table 1.

Differences arise from the problem that not all simulations are computational and that not all modelling represents a simulation, as discussed above (in particular, the increased application of statistical models may be responsible for these numbers).

Table 2 shows an overview of the 20 most characteristic terms for each congress (in terms of a high *tf-idf* score). The list still contains some obvious recognition errors from the scanned documents or noise from formulas or tables which have not been filtered out from the text. The studies of 1961–1967 seem to be concerned with physiology, voice and equipment. In 1971 the term "neanderthal" shows up [44]. The terms become thematically more diverse.

5 Discussion

The view appears to be spreading among phoneticians and phonologists that a formal model necessarily needs to be implemented. Johnson [45], for example, comments on one of his earlier models and points out the fact that "it wasn't an implemented model" which he sees as "one key problem". Only a computational implementation allows for a rigorous investigation of a model and its underlying theory. As Henke [46] pointed out almost half a century earlier: "[a model] must be 'implemented' so that its behaviour or 'outputs' for given inputs can be observed and compared with the real system. An unimplemented model cannot be so tested and thus seems quite empty of purpose." The question, whether computer simulations are a new kind of science or if they represent yet another kind of experimental research method is also discussed in the philosophy of science [cf. 47]. There, [13, p.595f] propose to see computer simulations within the continuity of the philosophy of science, instead of postulating something completely new. Accordingly, the recent rapid increase in computer simulation studies in phonetics and phonology is better appreciated as a continuation of a long tradition in our fields of research. While [13] argue that computer simulations are not something entirely new in the philosophy of science and stress their connection to other scientific approaches, [47] emphasizes their epistemic power and their role as explanatory devices.

6 Conclusions

A historic review of the literature on speech sciences shows that precursors to modern day computational models can be identified in mechanical and electronic "simulations" of human speech production. It can also be argued that simulations, as implementations of formal models, are also rooted in thought experiments.

A first attempt at a systematic literature review was presented. It shows that after hiatus in the series of the ICPhS, computational simulation studies had a constant albeit low share in the contributions to the proceedings. Note that this low percentage of simulation studies found in the ICPhS proceedings does not necessarily reflect their impact in the field. The increase in the total number of simulation studies is certainly related to the fact that computers became ever more powerful, smaller and cheaper as compared to previous decades.

A propose qualitative analysis presented here gives an impression of different thematic focuses over the years. The automatic analysis, however, suffers from missing digitized full texts of the early congresses.

7 Acknowledgements

This work is funded by the German Research Foundation (DFG), grants SFB 732 / A2 and SimPhon.Net.

References

[1] MOORE, R. K.: *Computational phonetics.* In K. ELENIUS and P. BRANDERUD (eds.), *Proceedings of the XIIIth International Congress of Phonetic Sciences*, vol. 4, pp. 68–71. 1995.

[2] TILLMANN, H. G.: *Three areas of computational phonetics.* In K. ELENIUS and P. BRANDERUD (eds.), *Proceedings of the XIIIth International Congress of Phonetic Sciences*, vol. 4, pp. 72–75. 1995.

[3] KOERNER, E. F. K.: *Historiography of phonetics: the state of the art. Journal of the International Phonetic Association*, 23(01), p. 1, 1993. doi:10.1017/S0025100300004710. URL `http://www.journals.cambridge.org/abstract_S0025100300004710`.

[4] ZWIRNER, E. and K. ZWIRNER: *Grundfragen der phonometrischen Linguistik.* Karger, Basel; New York, 3 edn., 1982.

[5] LIÉNARD, J.-S.: *From speaking machines to speech synthesis.* In *Actes du XIIème Congres International Des Sciences Phonetiques: 19-24 août 1991 – Aix-en-Provence, France*, vol. 1, pp. 18–27. 1991.

[6] STEVENS, K. N.: *The contribution of speech synthesis to phonetics: Dennis klatt's legacy.* In *Actes du XIIème Congres International Des Sciences Phonetiques: 19-24 août 1991 – Aix-en-Provence, France*, vol. 1, pp. 28–37. 1991.

[7] KÖSTER, J.-P.: *Historische Entwicklung von Syntheseapparaten zur Erzeugung statischer und vokalartiger Signale nebst Untersuchungen zur Synthese deutscher Vokale.* Helmut Buske Verlag, Hamburg, 1973.

[8] LOAKES, D.: *From IPA to Praat and beyond.* In A. KEITH (ed.), *The Oxford Handbook of the History of Linguistics*, pp. 123–140. Oxford University Press, 2013.

[9] MANNING, C. D. and H. SCHÜTZE: *Foundations of Statistical Natural Language Processing.* MIT Press., Cambridge, MA, 1999.

[10] FANT, G.: *Phonetics and speech technology.* In *Proceedings of the Tenth International Congress of Phonetic Sciences*, pp. 13–24. Foris Publications, Dordrecht, Holland ; Cinnaminson, U.S.A., 1984.

[11] THOMASON, S. G.: *Thought experiments in linguistics.* In *Thought experiments in science and philosophy*, pp. 247–257. Rowman & Littlefield Publishers, Inc., 1991. URL `http://philsci-archive.pitt.edu/3190/1/14_thomason.pdf`.

[12] OHALA, J. J.: *The segment: primitive or derived?* In G. J. DOCHERTY and D. R. LADD (eds.), *Gesture, Segment, Prosody*, no. 2 in Papers in Laboratory Phonology, pp. 166–183. Cambridge University Press, 1992.

[13] FRIGG, R. and J. REISS: *The philosophy of simulation: hot new issues or same old stew? Synthese*, 169(3), pp. 593–613, 2009. doi:10.1007/s11229-008-9438-z. URL `http://link.springer.com/10.1007/s11229-008-9438-z`.

[14] FAGYAL, Z.: *Phonetics and speaking machines: On the mechanical simulation of human speech in the 17th century. Historiographia Linguistica*, 28(3), pp. 289–330, 2001.

[15] BRACKHANE, F.: *“Kann was natürlicher, als Vox humana, klingen?” – Ein Beitrag zur Geschichte der mechanischen Sprachsynthese*. No. 18 in PHONUS. Institut für Phonetik, Universität des Saarlandes, Saarbrücken, 2015. URL http://www.coli.uni-saarland.de/groups/WB/Phonetics/contents/phonus-pdf/phonus18/phonus_18_brackhane.pdf. Doctoral dissertation.

[16] PAGET, R.: *The evolution of speech in men*. In [28], pp. 92–95.

[17] DUDLEY, H. and T. H. TARNOCZY: *The speaking machine of Wolfgang von Kempelen*. *The Journal of the Acoustical Society of America*, 22(2), pp. 151–166, 1950. doi:http://dx.doi.org/10.1121/1.1906583. URL http://scitation.aip.org/content/asa/journal/jasa/22/2/10.1121/1.1906583.

[18] TROUVAIN, J. and F. BRACKHANE: *Wolfgang von Kempelen's 'speaking machine' as an instrument for demonstration and research*. In [42], pp. 164–167. URL www.icphs2011.hk.

[19] OHALA, J. J.: *Christian Gottlieb Kratzenstein: Pioneer in speech synthesis*. In [42], pp. 156–159. URL www.icphs2011.hk.

[20] ARAI, T.: *Mechanical models of the human vocal tract*. *Acoustics Today*, 9(4), pp. 25–30, 2013. URL http://acousticstoday.org/issues/2013AT/Oct2013/#?page=26.

[21] GAUFFIN, J., S. GRANQVIST, and B. HAMMARBERG: *Irregularities in the voice: Some perceptual experiments using synthetic voices*. In [38], pp. 242–245.

[22] ALWAN, A., P. BANGAYAN, J. KREIMAN, and C. LONG: *Time and frequency synthesis paramters of severely pathological voice qualities*. In [38].

[23] R CORE TEAM: *R: A Language and Environment for Statistical Computing*. R Foundation for Statistical Computing, Vienna, Austria, 2016. URL https://www.R-project.org/.

[24] HORNIK, K.: *NLP: Natural Language Processing Infrastructure*, 2017. URL https://CRAN.R-project.org/package=NLP. R package version 0.1-10.

[25] WICKHAM, H.: *tidyverse: Easily Install and Load 'Tidyverse' Packages*, 2017. URL https://CRAN.R-project.org/package=tidyverse. R package version 1.1.1.

[26] FELLOWS, I.: *wordcloud: Word Clouds*, 2014. URL https://CRAN.R-project.org/package=wordcloud. R package version 2.5.

[27] MANNING, C. D., P. RAGHAVAN, and H. SCHÜTZE: *Introduction to information retrieval*. Cambridge University Press, New York, 2008.

[28] ANONYMOUS (ed.): *Proceedings of the International Congress of Phonetic Sciences*. Amsterdam, 1932.

[29] JONES, D. and D. B. FRY (eds.): *Proceedings of the Second International Congress of Phonetic Sciences*. Cambridge University Press, 1935.

[30] SOVIJÄRVI, A. and P. AALTO (eds.): *Proceedings of the Fourth International Congress of Phonetic Sciences*. Mouton & Co., 1961.

[31] ZWIRNER, E. and W. BETHGE (eds.): *Proceedings of the Fifth International Congress of Phonetic Sciences*. S. Karger, Basel, New York, 1965.

[32] HÁLA, B., M. ROMPORTL, and P. JANOTA (eds.): *Proceedings of the Sixth International Congress of Phonetic Sciences*. Hueber, Academia: Publishing House of the Czechoslovak Academy of Sciences, Chilton, München, Prague, Philadelphia, 1970.

[33] RIGAULT, A. and R. CHARBONNEAU (eds.): *Proceedings of the Seventh International Congress of Phonetic Sciences*. Mouton, The Hague, Paris, 1972.

[34] FISCHER-JØRGENSEN, E., R. JØRGEN, and N. THORSEN (eds.): *Proceedings of the Ninth International Congress of Phonetic Sciences*, vol. 1–3. Institute of Phonetics, University of Copenhagen, Copenhagen, 1979.

[35] BROECKE, M. P. R. V. D. and A. COHEN (eds.): *Proceedings of the Tenth International Congress of Phonetic Sciences*. No. 2B in Netherlands phonetic archives. Foris Publications, Dordrecht, Holland ; Cinnaminson, U.S.A., 1984.

[36] *Proceedings XIth ICPhS: The Eleventh International Congress of Phonetic Sciences*. 1987.

[37] *Actes du XIIème Congres International Des Sciences Phonetiques: 19-24 août 1991 – Aix-en-Provence, France*. 1991.

[38] ELENIUS, K. and P. BRANDERUD (eds.): *Proceedings of the XIIIth International Congress of Phonetic Sciences: ICPhS 95, Stockholm, Sweden, 13 - 19 August*, vol. 1–4. KTH (Kungliga Tekniska Högskolan, Royal Inst. of Technology) and Stockholm University, Stockholm, 1995.

[39] OHALA, J. J., Y. HASEGAWA, M. OHALA, D. GRANVILLE, and A. C. BAILEY (eds.): *Proceedings of The XIVth International Congress of Phonetic Sciences*. 1999.

[40] SOLÉ, M. J., D. RECASENS, and J. ROMERO (eds.): *Proceedings of the 15th International Congress of Phonetic Sciences*. 2003.

[41] TROUVAIN, J. and W. J. BARRY (eds.): *Proceedings of the 16th International Congress of Phonetic Sciences*. 2007.

[42] LEE, W.-S. and E. ZEE (eds.): *Proceedings of the 17th Intrnational Congress of Phonetic Sciences*. 2011. URL `www.icphs2011.hk`.

[43] THE SCOTTISH CONSORTIUM FOR ICPHS 2015 (ed.): *Proceedings of the 18th International Congress of Phonetic Sciences (ICPhS)*. International Phonetic Association, London, 2015. URL `https://www.internationalphoneticassociation.org/icphs-proceedings/ICPhS2015/proceedings.html`.

[44] LIEBERMAN, P.: *On the evolution of human language*. In [33], pp. 258–275.

[45] JOHNSON, K.: *Modeling phonology in time*. In *2011 Annual Report*, pp. 183–188. UC Berkeley Phonology Lab, 2011. URL `http://linguistics.berkeley.edu/phonlab/annual_report/annual_report_2011.html`.

[46] HENKE, W. L.: *Dynamic Articulatory Model of Speech Production Using Computer Simulation*. Ph.D. thesis, Massachusetts Institute of Technology, 1966.

[47] DURÁN, J. M.: *Explaining simulated phenomena: a defense of the epistemic power of computer simulations*. Doctoral Dissertation, Universität Stuttgart, Stuttgart, Germany, 2014. URL `http://elib.uni-stuttgart.de/opus/volltexte/2014/9265`.

Table 2. Highest scoring terms from simulation-related ICPhS papers.

year	*top 20 TF-IDF terms*
1961	diaphragm, eddies, inspiratory, cords, svend, mucosa, rubber, stroboscopic, cushion, pieces, ring, travelling, membranes, ove, reed, poles, painted, synthesizers, kc, belt
1964	cps, instrumental, cooper, instrumentation, caricature, ibm, manipulator, tomographic, wendahl, helsinki, truby, analyzer, cuts, electrodes, recorders, tape, analog, glottograms, keen, overpressure
1967	creak, nasalised, velarised, whispery, falsetto, blew, harshness, harsh, cis, wind, optional, museular, supralaryngeal, voiee, settings, abererombie, analysable, aooustic, approaeh, artifioial
1971	neanderthal, supra-laryngeal, lieberman, fossil, crelin, linguist, lafon, steinheim, man, nonhuman, paddock, scanian, newborn, generative, neutralization, jakobson, ls, halle, supralaryngeal, n-ary
1979	prog, technol, mosaic, gunnar, wakita, totallength, 2m, 1975a, painting, autonomous, discipline, 1975b, ambiguities, dosage, ekx, hisashi, bandwidths, prof, lpc, infiuence
1983	singing, maccurtain, broecke, fo, deposits, dobzhansky, fink, termites, hirano, folds, pillars, prigogine, skewing, vocabulary, titze, biology, genetic, flow, ug, 1982b
1987	d-type, auditory, resolutions, canal, soundtype, soundtypes, square-law, vsts, karjalainen, distortion, bark, f-space, l-type, x5, icassp-84, alternatives, schröder, v-type, x4, chords
1991	syntagma, kempelen, spu, demisyllable, pec, strands, nn, reed, sonorant, assibilation, controller, faber, phonotactical, voder, ms, adduction, klatt, secondary, rhythmic, jaw
1995	nodules, prototypes, stylization, plant, leak, equilibrium, sf, nodule, flmp, jaw, mpg, aobo, hoarse, articulator, aabb, facilitation, mns, perplexity, motor, f0
1999	pα, α, jitter, upsid, δz, ihc, arx, classi, meddis, 2p, ö, ø, allr, alr, hwr, mri, apex, vot, acceptability, workspace
2003	different, pauses, first, gdd, plp5, f0, agent, dbs, uvfp, z0, clash, hz, hlsyn, facial, imitation, aic, o2, robot, frication, gimel
2007	clo, wd, nrw, infrequent, growth, rel, normalised, exemplar, lenition, intsint, momel, v-to-v, agent, closed-loop, romanian, rp, praat, episodic, acuity, priming
2011	cvs, l2, sonority, l1, f0, mandarin, cci, clicks, qta, chinese, dopamine, env, f2“, ema, ipp, ssm, rmse, dutch, bwa, tone
2015	diana, e:, isi, deficit, aos, f0, a:, ooip, pentatrainer2, focus, rts, feedforward, persian, somatosensory, jaw-lowering, perioral, sas, ms, intercept, apraxia

Author Index